SITTING

the physical art
of *meditation*

Erika Berland

Somatic Performer Press, LLC
Boulder, CO

ISBN 978-0-9985876-0-8
Ebook ISBN: 978-0-9985876-1-5

10 9 8 7 6 5 4 3 2 1

For my teachers:

Chögyam Trungpa Rinpoche

Sakyong Mipham Rinpoche

and Bonnie Bainbridge Cohen

Contents

Part Three: Mindfulness of Body in Everyday Life

Exercises

Foreword

The simplest things are the hardest to do. Sitting on a meditation cushion sounds like it should be easy, but for many of us it is a journey of aches and pains. We discover that we do not know how to sit properly, much less sit still! This is a humbling discovery and the beginning of making friends with our body.

Fortunately, there are compassionate and articulate guides, such as Erika Berland, who have deeply immersed themselves in the art of sitting. Erika comes from excellent lineages of body-mind wisdom with such teachers as Chögyam Trungpa, Sakyong Mipham, Bonnie Bainbridge Cohen, Irene Dowd, and many others. Even more importantly, she is a practitioner who has been on this path herself for many years. So she writes from her own experience.

In the same way, this is a source book for you to work and play with. It is designed to empower you to explore your experience of body-mind harmony in your own way. Her book is a rich blend of traditions, so there is a wide variety of exercises to choose from. I invite you to engage these teachings to wake up your life with good posture and to inspire your posture with a good heart.

—Ashe Acharya John Rockwell

Introduction

"If you can raise good posture in your head and shoulders, then regardless of your living situation, you will feel a sense of joy."

—Chögyam Trungpa

When I was in my early twenties, I sat my first month-long meditation retreat. Because I was a professional dancer, I thought sitting cross-legged with an upright posture for days on end would be a piece of cake. After a week or so, I was in agony. Every part of my body hurt that could hurt. I remember thinking, *I'll never dance again!*

At the end of every sitting-meditation session, we were encouraged to wander off and explore the countryside for a short break and, strangely, I found that my body felt just fine. I realized that I was confronting and shedding years of habitual holding in my body, plus adding tension and stress by trying to be the perfect meditator with perfect posture. Ever since, I have been working with the posture of meditation as a practice of deep bodywork and psychophysical transformation—a practice that continues to alter my perceptions of who I am.

Working directly with the body can be an experience of deep relaxation, joy, and freedom.

At the core of this guide to the posture of meditation are practical, experiential exercises and techniques that you can continue to work with over many months and years. You are invited to integrate the basic principles into your practice, explore what is most effective, and tweak or alter the instructions to best support the changing state of your body and mind. For more than twenty-five years, I have been giving meditation instruction in the Shambhala Buddhist tradition and engaging with students at all levels of experience, from brand-new meditators to the "old dogs" with decades of experience. For many meditators, specific and detailed instruction in the sitting posture of meditation has often made the difference between the struggle to conform to an ideal posture and the ability to relax into the posture as a perfect expression of joy and freedom.

> The body has the power to shape the mind and the mind has the power to shape the body.

Implicit in the many Eastern traditions that emphasize meditation is the centrality of the body to the meditative journey and the power of posture to shape the mind. Years ago, I had a *Peanuts* cartoon pinned up on my studio door. In the cartoon, Charlie Brown stands with slumped shoulders, looking down at the ground while trying to explain to Lucy why he can't stand up straight. Finally, he says, "If you're going to get any joy out of being depressed, you have to stand like this." While we might not be as aware of the effects of our postural stance on our state of mind as Charlie Brown, it's easy to recognize how our body language, gestures, and posture impact our perceptions of ourselves.

Mindfulness-awareness practices can permeate our physical

tissues down to the cellular level with awareness and presence. Through meditation, we can actually alter our physical karma. And by adding a simple anatomically based instruction, such as finding the proper balance of the skull on the spine, we can enhance the body-mind integration associated with meditation, relieving physical pain as well as mental holding and distress.

> Physical discomfort in the meditation posture is a natural stage of the journey.

For meditators, it is common to experience a degree of physical discomfort at some point along the meditation journey. The posture of meditation can be challenging for advanced meditators as well as beginners. When we slow down enough to notice how we feel in our body and mind, our sensitivity is naturally heightened. We might notice all the extra tension we are holding in our shoulders or the uncomfortable feeling in our gut. It can be a bit like anesthesia wearing off after surgery—areas of our body that were relatively numb begin to awaken. Sometimes these new sensations can be experienced as discomfort or even pain. Regardless of how long we've been meditating, if we lack a sense of body awareness it is much more difficult to know how to relieve physical discomfort or change a debilitating posture.

The title of a well-known book on meditation by Sakyong Mipham states that the purpose of meditation is "turning the mind into an ally" and the same can be said for the body.[1] Turning our body into an ally or friend not only lessens the fear and judgment of our bodies that is so often a part of our inner dialogue, it also gives us the tools and awareness to shift habitual patterns of body and mind.

My hope is that the guided instructions in this book can be used in an exploratory way, not so much to "fix" every physical problem, but to discover a deeper sense of body-mind synchronization through inquiry and mindfulness that will benefit your meditation practice altogether.

Part One

The Ancient Wisdom of Meditation
Meets Somatic Education

1

The Somatic Approach

"Somatics is the field which studies the soma: namely, the body as it is perceived from within the first-person perception."

—Thomas Hanna

Somatics is a new field of study and research that emerged in the middle of the twentieth century, unlike the meditative tradition that has been developing over thousands of years—yet both disciplines are closely related in their emphasis on personal experience and a shared view of the relationship of body and mind. Philosophers, bodyworkers, movement educators, and artists were the first to formulate many of the techniques and practices of the new field.[2] Philosopher and teacher Thomas Hanna coined the word "somatic" in 1976 to refer to the body as the experienced or conscious body, in contrast to the objective, mechanistic view of the body as inherently separate from the mind and awareness.[3]

The somatic methods that I have found most effective in working with the posture of meditation are primarily based on the practices and techniques developed by pioneering somatic educator Bonnie Bainbridge Cohen and The School for Body-Mind Centering®.[4]I first met Bonnie in 1981 at a movement workshop in Boulder, Colorado.

We spent two days rolling around, crawling, playing, resting, and investigating our bodies and the environment with all our senses. What became evident to me during the workshop was Bonnie's almost uncanny ability to weave physiological and anatomical information with profound instructions on the mind's ability to access the body's wisdom and intelligence directly. The experience was revelatory.

A few years after that initial experience, I had another life-changing experience when I attended a workshop that Bonnie taught as part of a festival celebrating the Dalai Lama's visit to the United States. Called The Physical Art of Sitting, Bonnie introduced "embodied maps" of the body as ways to work with the posture of meditation. While I was enthralled with the physical and anatomical information, what inspired me most was Bonnie's view of the body and mind—a view that seemed completely in accord with what I had been studying as a student of meditation and Eastern philosophy. Just as meditators for thousands of years have cultivated a sophisticated science of the mind through first-person experimentation, as somatic educator and author Don Hanlon Johnson expresses, "Bonnie has found a method for systematically linking the information contained in the brilliant array of biomedical maps with the wealth of knowledge present in personal experiences."[5]

> Somatics and meditation both employ awareness as the key to joining mind and body.

Eastern thought and body practices, such as yoga and martial arts, profoundly influenced the early Western pioneers of body-mind education. Linda Hartley articulates the somatic view of Body-Mind Centering when she describes the distinction "between mind as it is generally used in Western terminology as the mental functions of storing and processing information, thinking, reasoning, envisioning, imagining, remembering, directing attention, and so on; and mind as awareness."[6] Awareness is the key word that refers to the immediacy of experiencing the synchronization of mind and body. It is awareness that comprehends the intrinsic nonduality of body and mind.[7]

In somatic training, it is awareness that infiltrates scientific anatomical and physiological principles and then transforms that knowledge into a powerful tool for healing and discovering the body's innate wisdom and well-being. Somatic education and contemplative meditation traditions both hold the view that body and mind are inseparable and that consciousness pervades the body. Both traditions rely on honing our awareness to greater and greater levels of subtlety in order to develop an intimate relationship with our body and mind. Somatic training and meditation techniques both rely on the premise that through cultivating awareness, our personal experience becomes the compass and guide toward further growth and change.

Bonnie Bainbridge Cohen's method, and the methods of other somatic educators, highlight these similarities between somatic techniques and the practices of the meditator. Essentially, they both share a methodology based on cultivating a practice of heightened body-mind awareness. This shared view is about cultivating awareness as the path to insight and knowledge, which leads to an experience of the inseparability of mind and body. In the next chapters, we will explore somatic techniques that will increase your personal experience and awareness of your body in the posture of meditation.

2

Experiential Anatomy and Embodiment

"I see the body as being like sand. It's difficult to study the wind, but if you watch the way sand patterns form and disappear and re-emerge, then you can follow the patterns of the wind or, in this case, the mind ... Mostly what I observe is the process of mind."

—Bonnie Bainbridge Cohen

One of the many unique gifts that Bonnie Bainbridge Cohen has contributed to the field of movement and somatic education is the expression, through imagery and awareness practices, of the different qualities, or "minds," that the many tissues and systems in the body have. As somatic psychologist Susan Aposhyan says, inherent in this is the "uncompromising belief that consciousness pervades all of the body."[8] Practically speaking, the ramifications of this view are that when we feel our bodies in movement or in a particular posture, we also experience a particular consciousness unique to that movement or posture. If we can directly experience our organs, bones, fluids, and muscles, these tissues of the body will express their unique qualities based on their function and form. For instance, when we can feel and locate in our awareness the actual anatomical heart, we experience the unique feeling, emotion, and wisdom embedded in the heart's tissues. This practice of embodying anatomical structures is one of the primary somatic techniques for effecting change in our body-mind.

Experiential anatomy is the study of the embodiment of all the major systems of the body. While each system has its unique role to play in the functioning of the body, each system also has a unique part to play in the practice and embodiment of meditation and the meditation posture. The skeletal system provides us with a strong structure and the proper alignment of our bones with the forces of gravity, while the muscular system supports the bones in a continual dance of contraction and release. The organ system enhances our posture through a sense of inner volume and softness, connecting us to organic authenticity and emotional vulnerability. The nervous system and endocrine glands regulate, organize, and integrate our entire body-mind into a cohesive whole. The circulatory system brings us a continual sense of flow, refreshment, and renewal. Our posture and ability to focus and stay present is a reflection of the balance or imbalance of all these systems.

The practice of experiential anatomy combines a cognitive, conceptual understanding of anatomy with direct subjective experience of the tissues that make up the body systems. The specificity and precision of this objective-subjective exploration helps unlock the knowledge inherent in our cellular, energetic being. When we bring awareness to an anatomical system or a specific tissue of the body, we are simultaneously contacting and affecting the energetic system. Our entire world, from the micro to the macro, is made up of energy. Some is visible, like light, and some is too subtle for our senses to perceive. In *The Subtle Body*, energy healer and author Cyndi Dale makes a number of connections between the physical body and the energy body, beginning with the statement that energy can be defined as "information that vibrates." She goes on to state that "In some respects, every cell and organ within the body is an energy body. Each receives energy. Each breaks down, metabolizes, and disseminates energy." In this way, "understanding subtle anatomy depends upon knowledge of physical anatomy … the physical body you will learn is an extension of the energetic body."[9] As you contact the various tissues of the body through the exercises in this book, you will have the experience of the *physical* quality of the tissue, the *mind* of the tissue, and the *energy* that radiates or vibrates from the tissue. An experience can dawn that is beyond habitual patterns, concepts, thoughts, and projections of our body-minds. True embodiment dissolves our perceived limitations and psychophysical habits, opening us to a creative river of limitless perceptions and feelings.

> Visualization is a powerful technique to change habitual patterns.

One of the principal techniques of Western somatic practices is the practice of visualization and the use of imagery. In the visualization practices of Body-Mind Centering, anatomical imagery is employed to affect the tissues of the body to respond in specific ways. While visualization practices have long been an integral part of many Eastern meditation techniques, the West has only more recently tapped into the power of mental imagery to affect the body-mind.

In the 1930s, physical education teachers and researchers Mabel Elsworth Todd and subsequently her protégé Lulu Edith Sweigard, used the term "ideokinesis"[10] to refer to the practice of visualizing through creative imagery in order to affect the body's sensory and motor pathways.[11] Through experimentation, they discovered that simply visualizing the body moving in specific patterns, without perceivable muscular effort or movement, could reprogram muscular responses—thereby releasing tension as well as creating more efficient movement patterns. More recent research via brain-imaging technology has revealed that mentally practicing a particular movement utilizes the same brain regions as the actual execution of the movement.[12] In the sports world today, ideokinesis and visualization techniques have become standard techniques to improve performance.[13] Visualization is a powerful tool to link mind and body and to program more efficient action.

While sports research has focused on performance and physical actions, ideokinesis has also been used to change habitual patterns of tension and imbalance in the body. By refraining from movement, we are inhibiting habitual body-mind responses and cultivating the possibility of new feelings, sensations, and movements.[14]

Somatic educator Irene Dowd led a functional anatomy class at Naropa University in an extended visualization practice intended to release the chronic holding and strain in our backs, which many of us dancers suffered from at the time. While we rested on the floor, Irene instructed us to imagine that our torsos were inside a slightly rumpled suit. We were to slowly and methodically iron out the wrinkles in the suit, putting our imaginary iron to work on every surface of the jacket. My back melted as muscular tension gave way to warmth, a tingling sensation, and a deep feeling of relaxation.

Visualization focuses the awareness and is a primary practice of directing intention. It changes habitual patterns of response in the nervous system, opening up new pathways of experience and perception.

While visualization is a gateway to a direct experience of the body, the act of visualizing is not necessarily the actual

Embodiment is a being process, not a thinking process.

experience itself. Bonnie Bainbridge Cohen makes a distinction between the cerebral cortex informing the bodily tissues that they exist through visualization and the bodily tissues informing the brain. She refers to this experience of direct sensing and feeling of one's bodily tissues as "somatization."[15] For example, the toe does not need the cerebral cortex[16] to know and feel its "toeness." While visualization can evoke a particular somatic experience, it is also possible for us to focus our awareness directly on the body's tissues and experience the consciousness embedded in those tissues.

According to Bonnie, "Embodiment is a being process, not a doing process, not a thinking process. It is an awareness process in which the guide and witness dissolve into cellular consciousness." By using the term "cellular consciousness," Bonnie is bringing our awareness to a kind of ground zero, an acknowledgment that all our cells are awake and consciously present. In fact, she goes on to say:

Embodiment is the cells' awareness of themselves. It is a direct experience; there are no intermediary steps or translations. There is no guide or witness. There is the fully known consciousness of the experienced moment initiated from the cells themselves. In this instant, the brain is the last to know. There is complete knowing. There is peaceful comprehension. Out of this embodiment process emerges feeling, thinking, witnessing, understanding. The source of this process is love.[17]

Gentleness and nonaggression are intrinsic to the body-mind.

When Cohen uses the word "love" to describe the essence of the embodiment process, she is pointing to the nonaggression and gentleness that is fundamental to the psychophysical makeup of all human beings. Chögyam Trungpa and other meditation masters call these our "enlightened genes" and the Shambhala Buddhist tradition calls the experience "basic goodness."

At this time in the West, we live in a culture with deep-rooted patterns of self-loathing, judgment, and negativity related to our physical bodies. We have a habit of constantly thinking that we are too fat, too thin, too ugly, and too old. Contentment and love are not necessarily qualities that come to mind when we relate to our bodies, if we relate to them at all. The practice of meditation and the development of the felt sense cultivate the nonaggression and gentleness at the core of our beings.

Sensing the body directly increases our access to feeling and emotion.

When we access the body directly through awareness, we feel more. We feel more physically and psychophysically. While the five sense perceptions of touching, hearing, seeing, smelling, and tasting are heightened and awakened through awareness, Buddhist psychology recognizes a sixth sense, the mental field, that coordinates and organizes the other five. This is also where you experience thoughts and emotions.[18] Body awareness can become a conduit or pathway to a greater variety of emotional textures and energies that enrich us as feeling, sensitive human beings. Through patterns of fear, distress, and trauma, many of us have closed off sensation to parts of our bodies, even to our physicality as a whole, in a vain attempt to numb ourselves to emotional feeling and the deep pleasure and pain of sensation.

As we meditate, we come back over and over again to the feeling of our bodies, our posture and the quality of our breath. When we can rest in the immediacy of sensation, we find some relief from the constant churning of discursive thoughts and the body becomes a powerful anchor for awareness practice. Chögyam Trungpa says in *Shambhala: The Sacred Path of the Warrior*:

> You sit down and assume your posture, then you work with your breath; tshoo, go out, come back to your posture; tshoo, come back to your posture; tshoo. When thoughts arise, you label them "thinking" and come back to your posture, back to your breath. You have mind working with breath, but you always maintain body as a reference point. You are not working with your mind alone. You are working with your mind and your body, and when the two work together, you never leave reality.[19]

The practice of meditation is at its core an embodiment practice. By suffusing the body completely with awareness, every bodily tissue and cell has the potential to become fully present and conscious. Working with our meditation posture becomes a deep and subtle journey toward full embodiment.

3

How to Use This Book

"To take this posture itself is the purpose of our practice."
—Suzuki Roshi

This book is arranged to maximize the integration of the experiential with the informative. Each chapter highlights a body system and that system's specific support for the sitting posture. For example, as you focus your attention on the skeletal system, you will learn basic anatomical principles that relate to the structure and role of the bones in weight-bearing and balance. Along with this information, each section will have specific, guided exercises and visualizations that help you apply the information directly to your posture. Each exercise is divided into three parts; an *intention* that includes the basic instructions of the exercise, a particular *sensory focus*, and a *contemplation* that supports your integration of the material.

It is not necessary to read the book in a linear fashion; each chapter can stand alone in your application, so feel free to skip around herein. The guided instructions can also be used as stand-alone summaries of the information that you can continue to refer to once you have integrated the basic material.

I have also included a chapter that focuses on common questions about the posture of meditation, along with suggestions on which body system or exercises might be most helpful.

I encourage you to use the guided instructions and illustrations both on and off the cushion. You might begin a period of meditation with a brief check-in with your posture, focusing on one or another of the guided instructions. If there are instructions that you particularly connect with, let those become familiar enough off the cushion so that in a period of practice you allow the anatomical imagery to enter your awareness for just a very brief time; a few seconds is really all that is needed before you return to your object of meditation, be it the breath, mantra, or visualization. By trusting that you can just "touch" or flash the image with your awareness and then let it go, you will counteract the tendency to solidify the imagery into a heavy-handed thought process or storyline. In fact, a well-known Tibetan meditation master has likened the practice of visualization to more of a "feelization." If you begin to labor over "getting it right," wonder if you are feeling anything at all, or try too hard to embody the image or visualization, you will quickly lose the connection to a direct experience of the body. Staying with your meditation practice and employing that one, simple "touch" can have an immediate effect on your postural alignment, release of excess tension, and overall sense of ease.

While I have been specific about the practice of visualization, I want to note that throughout the explorations, instructions, and exercises in this book, I will use the directive words, *feel, visualize, image, imagine,* and *experience* somewhat interchangeably. Although all of these have slightly different qualities and meanings, I will use them interchangeably because any of these active words can be a lever into a nondual experience of body-mind. In my own experience as a teacher, I've noticed that because we all learn uniquely, we respond quite differently to an instruction to *feel* something as opposed to *visualize* it, or to *imagine* rather than *experience*. Begin to notice how these words affect you and what words you tend to use in your own inner dialogue or contemplation. Feel free to substitute words that give you the most access to experiencing your body directly.

Another approach to the material is to take a period of time on the cushion to do a "somatic contemplation."[20] Set aside some time at the beginning of your meditation session to explore and work directly with your posture, applying the somatic imagery that resonates with you. Pay attention to emotions or stories that bubble up in your consciousness, as noticing these aspects of your experience can bring insight into habitual patterns of body and mind.

To contemplate is to "reflect deeply," uncovering understanding or meaning that was previously covered over and not clearly visible. The meaning that we discover in the layers of the body is beyond the words of the instructions or the images. It is a direct, felt experience. Our bodily tissues have history, and memories are stored in them as well as wisdom and insight. At some point in your contemplation, let go of the words or concepts and just rest in the physical and emotional feelings that have arisen in your body.

Working with your mind and body through the posture of meditation is a lifelong journey of discovery; therefore I encourage you to infuse your practice with the spirit of inquiry.

- What are you noticing about the tightness in your shoulders?
- What is that gnawing sensation in your gut?
- When your mind feels settled, how do you experience that in your body?

- When you are agitated, is that sensation concentrated in a particular part of your body?

While this practice is not so much about the seeking of answers, it is the openness to explore how we feel in our bodies that is central to working with the posture as a living, changing reflection of our mind. Because if we approach the posture as a position to be endured, figured out once and for all, ignored, or fixed, we limit the wisdom of the body from bringing insight and clarity to the mind.

4

Discovering Support

"In a sitting or standing position surrender the entire weight of the body to gravity, and yet remain as tall as you possibly can be."

—Will Johnson

In the *Posture of Meditation*, Will Johnson notes that the sitting posture "might appear as a kind of somatic koan."[21] This koan is the seeming paradox of the sitting posture—the ability to remain completely awake and alert while at the same time being utterly relaxed. For many of us, the feeling of releasing, letting go, and deeply relaxing is associated with lying down or sleeping. The posture of meditation demands that we cultivate a totally present, awake body-mind, along with a sense of effortlessness and ease. Fortunately, this paradox of "effortless effort" can be cultivated by embodying the natural intelligence of the body's basic physiological makeup.

Honed through millions of years of evolutionary trial and error, the human body has learned how to efficiently navigate the forces of gravity with minimal tension and struggle. If we have forgotten some of what the body has learned through the millennia, we can—with practice—rediscover our physiological inheritance and with it the ability to remain awake, alert, present, and relaxed.

One of the core issues related to the posture of meditation is the need to find support for our verticality, our ability to remain upright. The body cannot relax unless it feels fundamentally supported, just as the mind will not relax unless it feels basically safe and secure. A simple rule of self-preservation, this principle must be respected as a primal response. The challenge then is to find support that is dynamic and not fixed, alive and not static. When we understand the basic principles of anatomy and the forces of gravity acting upon the body, we gain tools to engage with the posture of meditation in an ongoing process of discovery and psychophysical transformation.

When we experience pain, excess tension, or stress in different areas of the body in the posture of meditation, the underlying issue is commonly a lack of support for the area in distress. This book offers a number of different techniques and guided exercises to explore this fundamental issue of locating support for the different tissues of the body. Some of the guided imagery will focus on addressing a particular area of the body directly. Other techniques will focus on shoring up support above or below the distressed area to repattern or heal the tension and stress. We will also explore support by bringing our awareness to the various systems of the body. The structure of the skeletal system supports us in a very different way than the organ system does, as do the muscle, fluid, and glandular systems. We encounter different emotional qualities of support when we feel into our bones, or our soft tissues, or even our fluids. Through this process, we are building support for the entire body-mind through the interconnection of all the systems. For example, when our skeletal system is properly aligned with gravity, our muscles are able to release excess tension and holding. Awareness of our organs provides internal support for our pelvis, ribcage, and skull. The fluids lubricate and bring nutrition to all of our systems and the glands modulate the nervous system to bring it into balance.

Chögyam Trungpa has said that mindfulness of body, which is one of the traditional practices of the Four Foundations of Mindfulness, "is connected with the earth. It is an openness that has a base, a foundation. A quality of expansive awareness develops through mindfulness of body—a sense of being settled and of therefore being able to afford to open out."[22] This is a beautiful description of the posture of meditation altogether. The feeling of settling is as much a physiological experience as it is a state of mind. As we relax into our structure and ground ourselves through our lower organs and bones, bonded to and supported by the earth, we can "afford" to open out. We can open across our hearts, gently reach our heads toward heaven, and feel the possibilities of touching and connecting to our world.

Part Two

The Path of Guided Practice

5

Making Friends with Gravity

"When you sit, you actually sit. Even your floating thoughts begin to sit on their own bottoms ... You have a sense of solidness and groundedness, and, at the same time, a sense of being."

—Chögyam Trungpa

A relaxed and aligned sitting posture reflects a dynamic balance between the downward moving forces of gravity and the upward moving forces that resist gravity. The body is equipped with basic reflexes[23] and nervous system responses that bring us into alignment with these forces of gravity and help us negotiate the verticality of the sitting posture. These primitive reflexes are integrated into the nervous system during the first two years of life. There are reflexes that bond us to the earth and its gravitational force, grounding us and providing us with a stable, supporting surface. And there are reflexes that assist us in resisting gravity so that we can "leave the earth," enabling us to achieve an upright and relaxed posture. Through the strength and integration of these reflexes, we can experience the body as a conduit between the stability and groundedness of the earth, our base, and the open, limitless qualities of the sky.

As a newborn, one of the first reflexes to develop concerns how the infant transitions from the more weightless, aquatic environment of the womb to the experience of gravity as it presses down on the infant's bodily tissues.[24] This reflex is stimulated by the touch and pressure of the supporting surface on the infant's body. The infant responds to the stimulus of the supporting surface by further releasing its weight into gravity. With little resistance to the gravitational forces acting upon its tissues, the child is drawn toward the earth.

The basic principle of this early reflex is that the more support we feel from the earth or our caregivers' arms, the more we can soften and yield into that support. And the more we can yield, the stronger and more supported we will feel as we develop. Jean Ayres, a pioneering sensory integration therapist, calls this "gravitational security," and she states that it is "the trust that one is firmly connected to the earth and will always have a safe place to be. This trust comes from sensing the gravitational pull of the earth and organizing these sensations so that one is on 'friendly' terms with gravity."[25] This experience of the forces of compression via gravity is the basis for grounding in the meditation posture.

You can practice the sensation of fully yielding to gravity by lying down in a comfortable spot on the floor or a hard surface and guiding yourself in the Yielding exercise.

Yielding

Intention: To release excess tension in the body by grounding your sitting posture in the firm, reliable, supporting surface of the earth.

- Lie down on your back on a firm surface with your knees bent and your feet placed flat on the floor. If you prefer, you can place a pillow under your knees so you can relax your legs and your lower back is supported.[26]

• Bring your attention to where your body meets the earth. Imagine the earth inviting your entire body to yield into its supporting surface.

• Like resting on a raft floating in water, the upward-moving, supporting surface of the earth cradles and holds you.

• Imagine your bones, muscles, organs, and fluids settling and releasing, like sand settling to the bottom of a container of water.

• Visualize the cells that make up your bodily tissues as having weight and feel them let go toward the undersurface of your body, where your body meets the surface of the earth.

• Allow your skin to soften and open up to the contact with the earth. Rest with this awareness until you experience a deep sense of yielding and recuperation.

Sensory Focus

• Notice the parts of your body that feel heavier than other parts.

• As you open to the sensations of contact, feel different sensations such as temperature, texture, and pressure.

• Yielding can have a passive quality of fully releasing into support. It can also have an active quality of "listening" from the places of contact. Notice the difference between passive and active yielding, and enjoy both.

Contemplation

- Experiencing the forces of compression via gravity is the basis for grounding physically and emotionally in the meditation posture. Learning to fully yield into the support of the earth is the basis from which our fully upright, human posture evolves.

Once you have discovered the deep feeling of recuperation and grounding by fully yielding to gravity, you are ready to engage the reflexes that resist the pull of gravity. As Bonnie states, "On the basis of this bonding with gravity or earth, we can then leave it."[27] In the developmental process, the compressive element—or movement toward the earth—always precedes the ability to resist or reach away from the earth. Another way to say this is that the forces of compression in the body actively support forces that enable the body to resist gravity. When developing infants discover that they have a stable surface to push against and that by pushing they can either locomote or bring themselves to a higher level such as sitting or standing, they begin to more actively push with their feet, hands, head, or tail (pelvic floor). When we actively push, as the forces move through our body, we find we are able to reach and suspend.

There are a number of reflexes called the *positive supporting reflexes* that offer an important counter to the yielding reflex we just explored. The positive supporting reflexes actively engage us in resisting gravity—without them we'd still be slithering on our bellies. These reflexes underlie all weight-bearing on the upper and lower limbs and the spine.[28]

Even though we will be using these reflexes primarily in the sitting posture, it is helpful to first engage them in a standing posture. You can activate them by bringing your awareness to where your feet meet the ground and visualizing the ground rising up to "meet your feet." As the ground rises under your feet, engage the soles of your feet in gently pushing downward, as if your feet were pushing toward the center of the Earth. Feel the force of the push move through your whole body, lengthening your spine to the top of your head.

To activate these reflexes in the sitting posture, practice the following Positive Supporting Reflexes for the pelvic floor, the head, and the hands.

Positive Supporting Reflexes

Intention: To tap into the underlying reflexes that support a fully upright sitting posture.

- In sitting posture, yield through your pelvis and tail into the supporting surface of your cushion or chair.

- Just as we visualized the earth rising up under us when we lay down in the yielding exercise, now imagine your meditation cushion or chair seat rising up under your bottom to offer support. Let that feeling of upward moving support travel through your body.

- Next pay attention to the surface of your palms where they rest on your thighs. Imagine your thighs rising up under the palms of your hands, offering your hands a supporting surface to yield to.

- Then very gently press your hands into your thighs and feel that movement travel through your arms, into your ribcage and shoulder girdle, and out the top of your head. Your hands will be helping to support your whole upper torso with a minimum of effort.[29]

- To further increase the sense of light suspension through your skull, try placing a hardcover book on your head and feel how your head reaches toward the book to support it. You can sit with the book on your head for a short period of time or even try walking with the book.[30] When you remove the book, you will feel your head float up effortlessly. The effort to balance the book and support its weight tones the deep muscles of the neck and spine and helps to align the skull properly on your spine. (Take care and do not attempt this if you have neck problems.)

Sensory Focus

- Feel a lengthening happen through your spinal column from your tail to the very top of your head.

- Feel the balance of downward moving forces through yielding in the lower body and the upward moving forces suspending your upper torso and head.

- If you practice with the book on your head, notice if your head feels lighter, as if it is "floating" upward with more ease when you remove the book.

Contemplation

- The meditation posture is the laboratory where the forces of compression and suspension meet: if they are successfully balanced one feels at ease; if not, we are subject to stress and tension.

In the following chapters, we will explore "making friends with gravity" through many of the major systems of the body. By approaching this theme in a variety of ways, I hope you will find some favorite exercises and images that resonate with you.

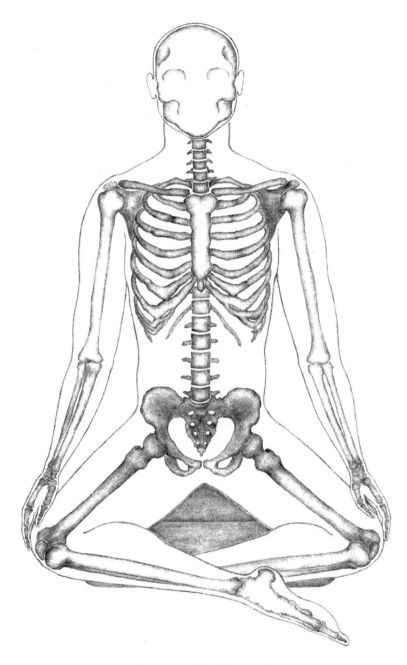

Figure 1: The Skeletal System

6

Dynamic Structure: Our Skeleton

"The ability to improve a pattern of support and movement for the reduction of mechanical stresses comes, not through the development of bulk and power in individual muscles, but from the study and appreciation of the body as a weight-bearing and weight-moving structure."

—Mabel Todd

When we place our awareness on our skeletal structure and allow weight to fall through our bones, we experience the compression forces and natural suspension forces that arise as the body's response to that weight. Our meditation posture naturally becomes more grounded, yet light and effortless. As our structure becomes more aligned with the forces of gravity, a topic we will explore in some depth in this chapter, the large muscle groups that are primarily designed to move the body in space can release and the deep, intrinsic postural muscles around the joints become more actively engaged in the support of our boney framework.

Qualities of Bone

The principle of "form follows function" is reflected in the evolution of the boney skeleton and our journey as a species from sea to dry land. Our bones and musculature developed primarily to resist gravity to the extent that we humans can, at this point, maintain a relatively effortless vertical posture. Bones resist gravity, but they also transfer the force or weight of gravity to the supporting surface, the ground, as efficiently as possible. In physics, the resistive force is called the *tensile* or *suspensive element* and the weight-bearing aspect is called the *compressive element*.

Any structural material such as bone, concrete, or steel must be stiff and hard enough to resist crushing under the weight of gravity. These are the uprights, or weight-bearing structures. Along with the downward movement of the compressive element, all structures must have an upward movement, or tensile force, that resists gravity. A stable structure seeks equilibrium and our skeletal structure, while primarily designed to absorb the compressive forces of gravity, is also composed of boney braces, struts, and arches that act to "direct weight to points on the uprights where it may be received and transferred to the ground advantageously."[31] The weight-bearing skeleton would collapse without the tensile elements such as the ligaments that bind bone to bone and the deeper postural muscles that resist gravity. Interestingly, the makeup of our bones is a combination of tissues with both compressive and tensile forces. Approximately seventy-five percent of living bone has mineral content, which is the weight-bearing part of the bone: strong, durable, and relatively stiff. The remaining twenty-five percent is connective tissue comprised of elastic, malleable, and even completely fluid tissues like the liquid marrow.[32] Because of these combinations of tissues, our bones embody qualities of heaviness, density, strength, and durability as well as lightness, fluidity, and even elasticity.

Pause reading for a moment to reflect on how you imagine your bones. Do you envision them as the dry, white, brittle bones that you might come across in a museum exhibit? Or do you visualize them as they really are: pink-tinged, the outer skin shiny and glistening, the inner compact bone strong but resilient like the branches of a healthy tree, the deep, fluid red and yellow marrow streaming within? When our body image changes, we experience our body in a new way, bringing a fresh, living quality to views that were merely habitual or culturally superimposed.

Because bones are designed to support the weight of gravity, they can actually weaken and lose their strength and malleability without a certain amount of gravitational stress. Therefore, in balanced alignment, the weight of gravity should be primarily distributed throughout our skeletal structure while minimizing the stress of gravity on the soft tissues of the body like the organs and glands. We will explore this principle in detail in the following sections on the relationship between the skeleton and organs.

The Spine: Our Central Axis of Support

If you have ever been to a country where you have observed women and men carrying extremely heavy loads on their heads, then you have seen the power, beauty, and grace of the four natural curves of the spine in action. While the notion of the completely straight spine is probably a holdover from the European, Victorian era, when any "curves" were suspect, many of us still carry this image internally. In essence, a completely straight spine is a weak spine since it is the balance of the curves that provides for maximum shock absorption. A straight spine is also an unresponsive and often rigid spine since the subtle spinal movements and undulations that are natural to the spine are inhibited.[33] This holding pattern exhausts us, putting undue strain on our musculature and even impairing the gentle flow of the cerebral spinal fluid that bathes our spinal cord and brings nutrients to the brain and nervous system.

As important as it is to keep the spine from becoming too rigid or straight, if the four curves are exaggerated or out of balance, the result can be excess compression into supporting muscle groups or even organs. When the skull, spinal column, and pelvis are in alignment with gravity, the density and strength of these bones are especially designed to accept and support the weight of gravity. This in turn takes pressure off the soft tissue (especially the organs) so that these softer, more vulnerable structures can fulfill their role of chemical and electrical processing, thereby maintaining the homeostasis of the body-mind.

As meditators, one of the first sensations we might become aware of is the amount of tension we feel in our backs and shoulders when we sit in the meditation posture. However we hold ourselves during the day might be in stark contrast to the "extreme verticality" of the meditation posture. When we first attempt the meditation posture, our back muscles might become tense and overworked in their effort to hold us upright to fight the forces of gravity. While some of our back muscles will have to gain tone and strength over time, it can be helpful to realize that the spine also has a front. Most of us imagine our spines to be somewhere in our back and we even colloquially refer to our spinal column as our "back." The truth is, anatomically, because of the spinal curves, a substantial part of the spine passes to the center of our plumb line[34] and sometimes even slightly into the front space of the body. Bringing awareness to the front of the spine will help balance the body in the sitting posture and can aid in releasing chronic back tension.

It is particularly important to become familiar with one's own central axis and the spine's essential weight-bearing function. With familiarity, we learn to trust more in the "feeling" of our spines and less in an idealized image of what we think a spine should look like.

Use the next exercise to become familiar with your spine. You can practice this unwinding of your spine a number of times until you can really visualize and feel your central axis and the weight of gravity being distributed equally through all the vertebrae.

Balance the Curves of Your Spine

Intention: To balance the natural curves of the spine and release tension in the back and neck muscles by bringing awareness and openness to the front of the spine.

- Begin in the sitting posture and then relax your body forward, curving your spine and releasing the weight of your head. Support your weight with your hands if you need to.

- Bring awareness to the fact that your spine is not just in your back but that it has a front surface. Shift your focus to the front of your spine and away from the backspace of your body.

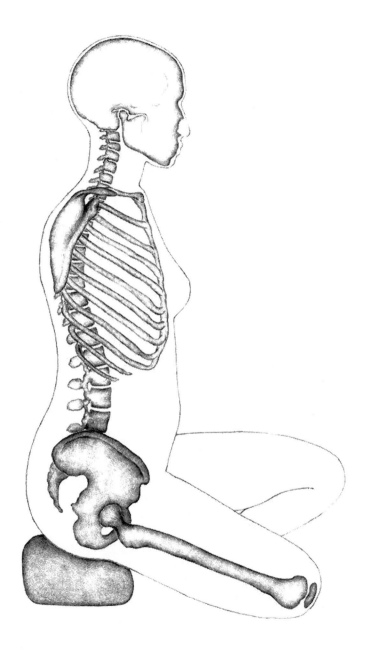

Figure 2: The Spinal Curves

- Now imagine a paintbrush moving up the front of your spine, brushing the front of your tail and proceeding up the entire length of your spine. As you paint, slowly unwind your spine, lengthening back to your vertical sitting posture.

- Release your tailbone toward the earth, imagining your tail as a long and heavy "dragon's tail" connecting you to the downward moving energy in your body.

- Visualize your skull as an extension of your spine, floating upward toward the sky. You are essentially "taking out the slack" in your spine, from top to bottom, through a gentle traction.

- Imagine placing a little bubble of air, or a soft bouncy gel pack, between any vertebra that feel especially tight or sticky.

Sensory Focus

- As you uncurl your spine, notice if you are initiating the movement from your back muscles, essentially "lifting" your spine. If so, try initiating the uncurling of your spine by focusing on lengthening and engaging the front of your spine rather than lifting from your back.

- Feel the power and solidity of the thick vertebrae of the lumbar spine (the curve in your lower back) as it curves toward the forward space of your belly. Open the front of your throat with its more delicate curve without dropping or collapsing the curve forward.

- Sense the downward moving energy in your body as you release your tail toward the earth. Feel the upward moving energy in your body as your skull reaches to "heaven."

Contemplation

- The uprightness of our posture reflects our ability to be fully present. According to Bonnie, in the process of infant development, their spinal movement patterns express the "mind of attention."[35] Imagine being in a movie theater and suddenly the film gets exciting. The spines of all those around you suddenly "snap to attention," as everyone sits up straight, eyes focused on the screen.

The Pelvis: Our Base of Support

In sitting posture, the pelvic girdle forms our base of support. It is composed of two pelvic halves, or hip bones, that are joined at the back to the sacrum via the *sacroiliac joints*, and in the front at the *pubic symphysis*. The top of the "wings" of the two hip bones are at our waist while the bottom of the hip bones is called our *ischium*—colloquially known as the "sitz" or "sitting" bones. The term "pelvis" usually includes the sacrum, although the sacrum is actually part of the spinal column.

In sitting posture, the weight is transferred to the two pelvic halves and slightly forward toward the pubic bone, or pubic symphysis, and into the cushion and legs. It can be helpful to think of each pelvic half as connected to the right or left leg, while the sacrum and tailbone remain a continuation of the spine. Many of us have patterns of "locking" the sacrum or tightening at the sacroiliac joints where the pelvic halves join the sacrum. Therefore, it is important to feel that the sacrum and tail are hanging freely while your weight is transferred toward your pubic bone and the front part of your sitz bones, which can be thought of as the "feet of the pelvis."

Establishing Your Seat

Intention: To establish a firm base of support for the sitting meditation posture through the even distribution of weight on the sitz bones and the maintenance of the natural curve in the lower back.

- Sit on your meditation seat and check that your knees are at the same height or slightly lower than your pelvic base. If your knees are higher then your seat and you've lost the natural curve in your lower back, raise your seat height with a support cushion.

- Place your hands on the top of each ilium at your waist. Slide your hands down into the crease at your hip joints until you can locate your pubic bone. Your pubic bone will feel that it is quite close to your cushion if your weight is centered toward the forward part of your sitz bones.

- Try rocking forward and backward on your sitz bones and then rock from side to side, alternately lifting one sitz bone at a time off the cushion. If you are having difficulty locating or feeling your sitz bones, try sitting directly on the floor or another hard surface for more direct feedback to this area.

- Now that you can initiate movement from your sitz bones, settle into a posture where most of your weight is falling slightly toward the front part of your sitz bones. If you have aligned your pelvis properly, you will notice that you have a natural curve in your lower back and your sacrum and tail are released.

Sensory Focus

- When you practice rocking on your sitz bones, sense the rocking movement being initiated directly from your sitz bones and not your lower back. If this is not clear, rock your pelvis forward and backward by actively bending and extending your lumbar curve and then notice the difference in sensation from initiating with your sitz bones. This is helpful to distinguish because when the sitz bones are more active in supporting our seat, the lower back can release any excess holding.

- Feel the sensations and feelings that arise when you rest your awareness on your sitz bones, acknowledging that they are the basis of support for establishing your "seat" in the meditation posture.

Contemplation

- When we can fully yield into our base of support, our bodies and minds feel more grounded. We bond with the solidness and reliability of the earth, giving us the ability to "hold our seats" in the midst of change and uncertainty.

The Shoulder Girdle and the Rib Cage

The shoulder girdle can be compared to a yoke that is hung across the top of the ribcage. The front of the yoke is composed of the two *clavicles*, the bones at the base of the neck that are connected to the *sternum*, or breastbone. The back of the yoke is made up of our shoulder blades. It is similar to the image we might have of a Dutch milkmaid attempting to balance her pails of milk by being careful to keep her yoke steady and upright.[36]

If we imagine ourselves as the Dutch milkmaid, we might ask ourselves if we are balancing our milk pails properly. Or are we spilling milk? More often than not, we will notice that our shoulder girdle is tipped slightly forward. Over time, that forward tilt will inevitably put strain on our neck and shoulder muscles. Sitting in low-slung chairs and hunching over computers, it is easy to find ourselves with habitually round shoulders, where our collarbones collapse forward and the back of our neck and shoulder muscles struggle to resist the pull of gravity. If you stand with your arms by your sides and your palms face backwards (rather than facing the sides of your body), this could be an indication that your shoulder girdle is tipped slightly forward and not properly aligned with the forces of gravity.

During meditation, in an effort to "sit up straight" and find our "head and shoulders,"[37] we often adjust our posture by lifting and pushing our ribcage up and out, military style. This tends to overwork the large muscles of the back and chest, tighten the diaphragm, and impact the quality and ease of our breath. To avoid this compensation, it is important to feel that the shoulder girdle can move quite independently of the ribs. In other words, if you have lengthened your spine and balanced your shoulder girdle properly, your ribs should be able to hang easily off of the spine. In the same way, while we colloquially refer to the ribs as a "cage," each rib is jointed to the spine in the back and the sternum or breastbone in the front, allowing for the free movement of each individual rib. The movement of the ribs can be likened to those of a "bucket handle." As we breathe, each individual "bucket handle" moves up and down, and the whole diameter of the rib cage expands and decreases.

Shoulder Girdle and Rib Cage Alignment

Intention: To align the shoulder girdle and rib cage with gravity and cultivate more effortless suspension of the upper body.

- Lift your shoulders up and down a few times to release any excess tension, then let the yoke of your shoulder girdle settle on top of your rib cage.

- Feel the tip of your shoulder blades sliding down your back as your collarbones gently rise to help align the shoulder girdle. You can imagine a little anchor hanging off the bottom of each shoulder blade, weighing them down as your collarbones float up.[38]

- To further differentiate the rib cage from the shoulder girdle, place your hands on your ribs and feel the movement that is occurring as you breathe. Notice if you have a habit of lifting your shoulders when you inhale. If so, remind yourself that the ribs can move independently of the shoulders and that there is no need to engage the shoulder and neck muscles, especially with quiet breathing.

- With your hands placed on your lower ribs, as you breathe feel each "bucket handle" move up and down, as the whole diameter of the "rib cage" expands on the inhale and releases on the exhale.

- Sit in meditation posture and feel the balance of your shoulder girdle front to back, with the tips of the shoulder blades sliding down your back and the collarbones gently floating upward. Your ribs can feel as if they are gently sloping off your spine with no need to hold or thrust your chest up and forward.

Sensory Focus

- To clearly differentiate the ribs from the shoulder girdle, practice making large circles with your arms and notice the feeling of your shoulder blades as they glide on your upper back. Your ribs remain restful, gently moving with your breath.

Contemplation

- What does it feel like to be lifted and supported in your upper body as you go through your day? Does it feel exposed, safe, open, expansive, or scary? Contrast that experience with rolling your shoulders forward or pushing your scapula down and lifting and thrusting your chest out. What are the mental and emotional qualities of those postures?

With the pelvis as our firm base of support, our upper body—chest, arms, and head—is able to suspend and lift with less effort. When our upper bodies expend less effort trying to hold ourselves upright, there is a natural opening and widening across the chest. With good structural support, we might notice that the area around our hearts is more able to radiate and expand.

The Skull

Just as proper alignment of the shoulder girdle can release chronic neck and shoulder tension, the proper placement of the skull on the first vertebra, or *atlas*, is key to avoiding a buildup of tension throughout the body.[39] The skull and brain weigh between ten to twelve pounds and, if not aligned properly on the spinal column, the imbalance creates tremendous stress in the muscles of the neck, shoulders, and back. The relatively new phenomenon of "text neck," where the forward angle of the head on the spine is increasingly creating neck problems and even headaches, is a testament to the importance of head-neck alignment.

The bottom of the skull has two rounded protrusions, or *condyles*, that sit in the two sockets of the first spinal vertebra, or atlas. They rock on the atlas if we are nodding our head. This is similar to the bottom of our pelvis, where we explored the balance of the sitz bones on our seat. The skull's "sitting bones" are supported by the atlas at the *atlanto-occipital joint*. This joint is located just below the level of the bottom of our earlobes and approximately at the same level of the *temporomandibular joints (TMJ)*. The TMJ are located at the junction of your jaw and skull. If you place your fingers in the small indentations of your TMJ, you can feel them when you open and close your mouth or move your jaw side to side.

Use these guided instructions to explore the most efficient balance point for your skull on your spine.

Align Your Skull on Your Spine

Intention: To balance the skull in line with gravity so that the shoulder, neck, and back muscles can release excess holding and stress.

- Place your fingers on your TMJs and gently initiate a very small rocking motion of your skull as it glides in the sockets of the atlas. Resist initiating the movement of the skull from your neck; instead focus on making the rocking happen at the level of your jaw joints.

- When you can feel the movement occurring at the atlanto-occipital joint where skull and spine meet, remove your fingers from your jaw and simply nod your skull like a bobblehead doll. Take care not to initiate this movement in your neck. Cease the bobbing movement when you can sense that the bottom of your skull is resting right in the center of the two sockets, or condyles, of the atlas.

- Feel that the shape of the over-curve of the back of your skull is as present in your awareness as the front of your skull or face. Your chin will be slightly dropped, but not as the result of any movement or adjustment in your neck.

- You can check that the tip of your earlobe is in line with the very edge of your shoulder girdle but take care not to over-straighten your neck to achieve this alignment. It might help to balance a book on your head for a few moments, as instructed in the Positive Supporting Reflexes exercise, to feel the proper balance.

Sensory Focus

- Sense where the rocking action of the skull on the atlas is actually taking place. You might be surprised that the perception of where your spine ends and your skull begins is quite different from what you had imagined. If you lengthen your spinal column and bring awareness to this atlanto-occipital joint, you may notice how long your neck feels and that your head is balanced quite high up on your spine.

Contemplation

- The tendency we have to reach forward with the head is, in some sense, natural since the special senses of the eyes, nose, and tongue are all located in the front space of the skull. We are literally reaching out with our perceptions. Letting go of that tendency to overreach can help us feel more centered in our body and our awareness. During your daily activities, notice if you are habitually reaching your head forward or downward and pause to connect with the emotional feeling of the habit. Notice if you have a change of "mind" when you reestablish the balance of your skull on your spine.

The frequent instruction given in meditation posture to "tuck the chin" is often misunderstood because when we actively tuck the chin, we tend to straighten the neck—thereby inhibiting its natural curve. Over-straightening the neck can result in compression of the spinal discs and muscle tension that affects breathing, circulation, and the movement of energy through the throat. The instruction to "tuck the chin" is often offered as an antidote to the habitual pattern many of us have of thrusting our head and chin forward, resulting in an exaggerated curve in our necks. This is sometimes referred to as "forward head" and is the opposite, although equally problematic pattern, of "text neck" where our head is dropped. It is important to understand that the intention of the instruction, while easily misunderstood, is to keep the neck soft and open, and to balance the condyles of the skull on the atlas.

Alignment Markers

You can integrate the proper alignment of the pelvis, shoulders, and skull by checking specific boney landmarks that correlate with a skeletal structure that is efficiently aligned with gravity in the sitting posture.

First, notice the outer edges of your shoulders where, if you were wearing a military uniform, your epaulets might be. See if they are in line with the top of your hip bones, or *illiac* crests. Next, check if the tip of your earlobe is in line with the tip of your shoulder girdle. You might need to have a friend help you with this or you can attempt to get a side view of yourself in a mirror.

If you notice that these skeletal landmarks are misaligned, engage your curiosity. You can gently question why your head might be placed forward of your shoulder girdle. Are your special senses, the eyes, ears, and mouth pulling you forward off of your center of gravity? Are you straining to see something? Are the chairs and car seating that you use supporting the curve in your lower back or are they forcing you into a C-curve so that the integrity of the four curves of your spine is lost? Most importantly, as you become aware of these reference points, don't force a "correct" posture but maintain an attitude of curiosity and gentleness as you continue to explore your alignment.

Feeling into a New Alignment

Becoming curious about the body-mind connection and the interrelationship of our posture with our thoughts, emotions, and state of mind opens us up to further possibilities for change. What do you notice about the "mind" of your posture? Is there a slight feeling of depression (like the example of Charlie Brown in the Introduction), so that your chest is dropped and your shoulders roll forward? Are your shoulders behind your hips and your chest thrust forward in a military posture that expresses a feeling of overconfidence or a lack of vulnerability?

When you can inquire about the relationship of your state of mind with your posture, you can then very gently and slowly begin to feel into a "new" alignment. I use the word "feel" because rather than simply adjusting your head, shoulders, or pelvis to the "correct" alignment, you will have more success if you join the visual image of correct alignment with the feeling in your body and mind as you make small, micro-changes toward that image. If we merely adjust the parts of the body to be where we think they should be, the effort to hold that posture will quickly overwhelm and exhaust us, making any postural changes unsustainable. Sometimes the process of changing our alignment can feel like a subtle "unwinding" or "growing" into a new form. The key is staying with the sensations that are occurring as you move toward more efficient skeletal alignment.

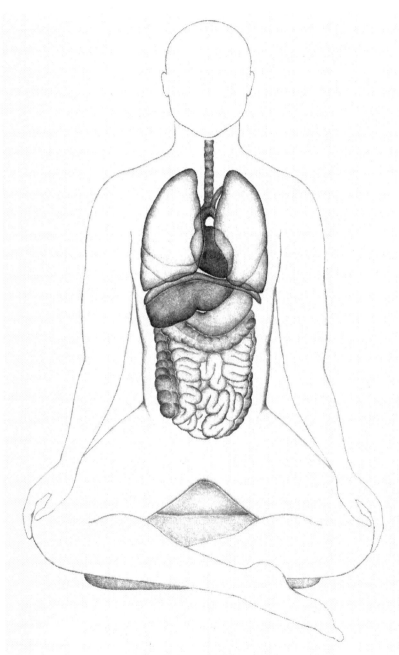

Figure 3: The Organ System

7

Soft Underbelly: Our Organs

"The organs provide us with a sense of volume, full-bodiedness, and 'organic' authenticity."

—Bonnie Bainbridge Cohen

We have been exploring the skeleton as the primary structural support for the transfer of weight through the body in the meditation posture. Imagine though, for a moment, that all of your organs are like water-filled balloons, with the outward pressure of the water gently pressing against the skeletal structure from the inside of your body. If those balloons suddenly deflated, your skeletal structure would lose some of its integrity and collapse in on itself. The soft, mostly fluid-filled organs provide us with an inner counterforce that supports our posture from the inside out.

In addition to their internal support, Bonnie points out that "Organs are the primary habitats of emotions, aspirations, and the memories of our inner reactions to our personal histories."[40] As emotional storehouses, they connect us to our gut feelings and to our deep, emotional core.

Our language is filled with rich expressions of the intuitive connections between organs and emotions. One can accuse someone of having "some gall" or being "full of bile"; you can "vent your spleen" or "not have the stomach" for this or that. And then there are the numerous expressions related to the heart: "softhearted," "brokenhearted," "heartfelt," and "hearty," to name just a few.

Sensing your organ body when you are meditating helps cultivate emotional authenticity so that meditation practice opens you fully to all aspects of your being. The posture of meditation also provides an opportunity to relax and release the organs, as organs can hold tension just like muscles. It also enlivens them, giving them room to breathe and expand. To fully embody these soft, internal structures, first practice connecting with your organs lying down and then proceed to incorporating their qualities and images into your meditation posture.

Connect to Your Organ Body

Intention: To access internal support for the skeletal structure and to open pathways to feeling and emotion in the meditation practice.

- Lie on your back with your knees bent (you can place a pillow under your knees for more support) and place your hands on your belly. Allow your lower organs to fall back into the whole bowl of the pelvis, like water settling to the bottom of a container.

- Feel your breath rising and falling beneath your hands. Visualize that a ripple-like massage occurs in the soft tissue with the filling and emptying of each breath.

- Spend a few minutes focusing on your digestive organs,

visualizing the breath filling and emptying into the continuous space that runs from your mouth through your throat to your stomach into the hollow intestines and out your rectum and anus.

- Now move your hands to any organ that is calling you, visualizing the filling and emptying of your breath in specific organs such as the bladder, uterus, pancreas, heart, and even your brain. With each breath, feel the organ gently expand and then release.

- Having softened your organs, very slowly roll to your side and feel, as you roll, how the organs respond to the pull of gravity, allowing them to fully release. Change your position a few times, rolling onto your belly or onto your other side, initiating the movement from the release and weighty quality of the organs yielding to gravity.

- Eventually bring yourself to a sitting posture and, as you do, feel the internal realignment of your organs with gravity. In the sitting posture, release the lower organs in the pelvic bowl toward the earth while feeling the lightness of the upper organs of the heart and lungs gently suspending and offering support for your ribs and shoulder girdle.

Sensory Focus

- Feel the softness and pliability of your insides as they continually mold themselves and shape-shift in response to gravity, breath, and movement.

- In the sitting posture, notice if you are tightening in the belly area, as this will impede the natural massaging of the organs, the movement of the diaphragm, and, in turn, the freedom of the breath.

- Listen to the feelings and emotional textures that live in your organs.

Contemplation

- When we slow down enough, we can begin to notice our relationship to our organs. The organs reveal our relationship to processing and integration. How do we digest information? How do we circulate information and energy through our bodies? Do we even acknowledge that we have "insides"? Are we in touch with the messages our organs constantly give us about the state of our body-mind, or do we override them in service to an external goal?

The lower organs, the contents of the pelvic bowl, include the reproductive organs, the bladder, and the large and small intestines. Just as we felt the pelvis to be our "seat" or base—grounding us and lowering our center of gravity—the movement and energy of the lower organs connects us to our legs and feet and how we move upon the earth. As you bring awareness to your lower organs in the sitting posture by releasing them into the pelvic bowl, you might feel a deep sense of contentment, like a baby after nursing. Our digestive organs in particular embody qualities of self-nurturance and with their connection to what scientists now call the "gut brain," an intuitive sense of safety and security.[41] The entire digestive system can be a reflection of the time it takes for each one of us to fully "digest" and process our experience.

The middle organs of the body such as the liver, stomach, pancreas, and kidneys create a band of support tucked under the dome of the diaphragm and at the base of the ribcage in the front, sides, and back. These organs act as a bridge between the upper and lower body and are intimately connected to the breathing process through the massage-like movement of the diaphragm as it gently presses on these organs with each inhalation and exhalation.

The Kidneys and Lower Back

Because of daily stress, we might not realize that we are going through our day holding our breath or breathing very shallowly. If this is the case, the middle or "bridge organs" mentioned previously, along with the diaphragm muscle[42] can become areas of unconscious tension and holding. We might also have a tendency to stabilize and immobilize this middle area of the body because of a lack of support either from below (our pelvic seat) or above (our ribcage and skull). With this lack of support, the middle organs begin to hold when they should be a free and flexible "bridge" between the grounding forces moving through the lower body and the suspension forces of the upper. The kidneys, located in the small of the lower back, are particularly vulnerable to a buildup of tension and immobility. This is in part because the kidneys are capped by the adrenal glands and these glands play a major role in our regulation of stress and metabolism. The adrenals release chemical hormones directly into the bloodstream in response to signals from our autonomic nervous system.[43]

Imagine stumbling into a bear in the middle of the woods—instantly, a rush of adrenalin would course through your body, alerting you of possible danger. This hormonal reaction mobilizes us for "fight or flight or freeze" responses, which is the nervous system helping us survive a potentially life-threatening situation. Whether or not we actually encounter a life-threatening situation, our body can remain primed to respond with adrenalin due to stressful thought patterns or emotional triggers. We can find ourselves locked in a pattern of what is commonly referred to as a "physical stress response." This habitual response can take a toll on our kidney-adrenal complex and can even be associated with lower back pain. There has been much written about the psychosomatic origins of some low back pain and its relationship to stress in general.[44] If we can bring awareness to unconscious habits of holding the breath or gripping and tightening in the kidney-adrenal area, then the meditation posture becomes a wonderful opportunity to repattern the stress response by working directly with the body-mind connection.

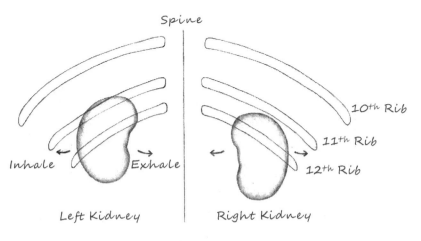

Figure 4: Breathing into the kidneys

Release the Kidneys and Lower Back

Intention: To release the tendency to hold and stabilize our posture by tightening the lower back and kidney area.

- Lie on your front with a support cushion or bolster under your belly and release your weight into the supporting surface. The pillow under your belly will help you to release your lower back.

- Breathe into the two kidneys that are located on either side of your lumbar curve and are approximately four inches long, two inches wide, and one inch thick. Imagine the kidneys widening away from your spine as you inhale and releasing back toward your spine as you exhale. As you breathe, you are visualizing the kidneys moving toward and away from your spine, side to side.

- After you have visualized and felt the kidneys being moved by the breath, shift your awareness to the subtle movement of the kidneys that is occurring independently of the breathing process. Because the primary role of the kidneys is to process and purify the fluids in our bodies, you can imagine the kidneys as little boats, bobbing, rocking, and responding to the fluid waves moving in and out of the kidneys. Rest in this natural flow of fluid and organ.

- Once you have experienced your kidneys in this supportive posture, try bringing a flash of awareness and breath into the kidney area when you are practicing sitting meditation. Visualizing the kidneys moving and breathing can have the immediate effect of softening and releasing the tendency to grip and control in this area.

Sensory Focus

• The kidneys love attention. Focusing on the fluid and tender quality of the kidneys with the gentle, aware embrace of the breath is very healing for them.

• Notice if you are trying too hard to initiate movement from the kidney area. It is easy to mistake contracting the lower back muscles for the more subtle gliding and sliding of the kidneys underneath the muscles. Rely on the visualization to effect changes in the tissue rather than actively trying to make something happen.

Contemplation

• Bring mindfulness to everyday habits of stress and notice if you can become aware of tightening or holding in your kidneys and lower back. Connect your emotional feeling with the physical holding as a way to begin to change the habitual pattern of tightening this area.

___

We have touched on the lower organs, connecting them to the sensation of grounding in the body and we've worked with the kidneys as a "supportive bridge" between the upper and lower body. Now, as we bring attention to the upper organs, in particular the lungs and heart, we will explore how they provide internal support for the rib cage and shoulder girdle. The lungs in particular provide lightness, suspension, and buoyancy. The heart, nestled between the lungs, is a central organ of upward support for the chest and ribcage.

The Lungs

The lungs fill the entire rib cage and are divided into lobes, which are natural indentations or sections where the tissue folds in on itself, providing more surface area for the lungs to expand. On the right side of the body, filling the ribcage, there are three lobes, while on the left there are only two, as the heart takes up some of the available space. The upper lobes of the lungs extend into the base of the front and back of the neck. The middle area wraps around from the front of our upper chest to just under our armpits. The lower lobes in the front extend down to the fifth and sixth ribs and in the back of our ribcage they slope down from the shoulder girdle and *scapula* to the very top of the kidneys and the floating ribs. The heart is partly covered by lung tissue in the front, reflecting the lung's intimate relationship with the heart, which is responsible for bringing the breath of life to the heart in the form of oxygen-rich blood.

Lung tissue is dense but light and sponge-like, made up of tiny little sacs, or *alveoli*, that expand with each inhalation, and soften and release with each exhalation. Like a sponge in water, the breath is naturally and effortlessly drawn into the lungs. As the alveoli fill with air, like millions of miniature balloons, the lung tissue can support and lighten the weight of the shoulder girdle and rib cage. This dense but light tissue provides gentle buoyancy from within the container of the rib cage to help suspend and support the upper body.

Like any part of the body, we can have areas that feel awake and fully engaged and other areas that feel numb or underutilized. Nowhere is this more apparent than in the lungs—we might find that there are whole areas where we are simply not breathing. With intention, we can distribute the breath throughout the lung tissue, gaining more lung capacity and effortless support for our entire rib cage and shoulder girdle. If we practice a guided somatic meditation with our lungs while lying down, when we move to the sitting posture we might feel that our upper body feels more supported from the inside out.

Energize Your Lungs

Intention: To increase internal support for the rib cage and shoulder girdle and cultivate an efficient and easeful breath pattern that reduces habitual tension related to our breathing process.

- Lying on your back with knees bent, place one or both hands on the upper lobe of your right lung. Tune in to the feeling of movement beneath your palms. You are feeling living lung tissue, expanding and releasing, filling and emptying. Feel how your skin, muscles, and ribs expand to accommodate the filling of the air sacs in your lungs.

- Move your awareness to the middle lobe, under your armpit and in your breast area. As you breathe, focus on the width of the lung as it expands into the side-space of your body and moves against your ribs. Apply the same effortless quality to the filling and emptying of the breath as you did for the upper lobe.

- Bring your awareness to the backspace of your body and the area of the lower lobe. As you inhale, fill the lower lobe with breath and feel how it moves against the back ribs, all the way down to the floating ribs and just above the kidneys. Stay with the intention to allow the lung tissue to expand and spread into the floor with each inhalation and to release and let go on each exhalation.

- Repeat this sequence on your left side, taking note that even though there are only two lobes, compared to the three lobes of the right lung, there is still a middle section of the lung that you can breathe into and explore.

- After you have completed both sides, take time to breathe into both the right and left lungs altogether. Explore the relationship of your arms and shoulders to your lungs. As you circle your arms or move them around, feel their natural connection with your lungs and your breath.

- Now sit back on your meditation cushion and notice how this exploration might have affected the quality of your support in the sitting posture. Have your back and chest muscles softened a bit? Does your upper body feel a little lighter? Does your breathing itself feel a bit more natural and less effortful?

Sensory Focus

- Notice where you feel at ease with your breath and where there are areas of your lungs that feel "sticky" or underused.

- Pay special attention to the quality of how the air enters the lung tissue. Rather than feeling that you need to "pull" the air in, you can imagine simply opening the membranes of the air sacs to "receive" the breath.

Contemplation

- Adopt an attitude of non-doing as you breathe. Breath and movement occur naturally, without effort. Simply tune into that process to awaken the special qualities of the lungs: ease, lightness, inner support, inspiration, and the strength of your life force. You are releasing tension, clearing your body of stagnancy, and cultivating the ability to let go.

The Heart

In Eastern thought and medicine, the heart is generally considered the seat of consciousness and awareness, while the West tends to locate consciousness primarily in the brain.[45] Regardless of cultural orientation, for most human beings the heart holds a wealth of imagery as reflected in the language and symbols that we associate with it. We are "heartsick," we have "loss of heart," we are "heartened," or our experience is "heartfelt." Feelings of compassion and love, or the lack of compassion and love, are all expressions of the heart. When we feel our hearts, we have the sense that we are touching into our truth and our "heart's desire." When we put our hands on our heart, we touch our human goodness, vulnerability, and deep desire for happiness. When we "give our heart" to others or when we are genuinely "openhearted," we extend those same feelings we have for ourselves to others.

The anatomical heart has its own blood supply, nerves, and glandular tissue and it beats tirelessly throughout our lives, very rarely missing a beat. The main *aorta* that carries freshly oxygenated blood to the whole body arches upward out of the heart toward the clavicle at the base of the neck. Like a fountain, the blood is muscularly pushed out of the heart into the aorta and carried through the rest of the body via the *arteries* and the even smaller *arterioles*. This sense of uplift, vitality, and fluid power can be felt to support the gentle suspension of the front of the chest and sternum. The blood is returned to the heart by way of tiny *venules* and *veins* that eventually empty into the *vena cava* and the heart. The movement of the blood back to the heart gives us a sense of self-nurturance and a return to "home base."

Energetically, the hands and wrists are connected to the heart. It is through our hands and arms that we reach out to others—it is our hands that pull others toward us and allow us to embrace them closely, heart to heart. Our hands are the physical expression of what our heart wants to say.

When we sit in the meditation posture we can feel a triangle of energetic support from the palms of our hands to our heart.

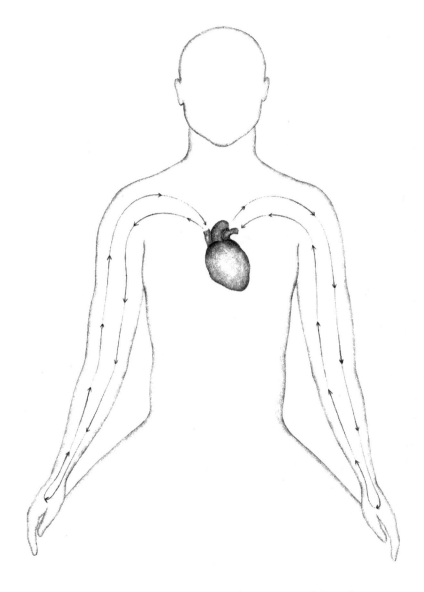

Figure 5: Connecting the Heart and Hands

Heart and Hands

Intention: To feel the connection and flow between the heart and the hands in the meditation posture.

- Sit with your hands on your thighs and bring attention to the feeling of your palms touching your thighs.

- As you release the muscles and bones of your hands onto the supporting surface of the thighs, feel an energetic uplift from your thighs into your hands.[46] Then gently press your hands toward your thighs and allow that feeling to flow up your arms and into your heart. Feel a triangle of support between your hands and your heart.

- If you have a habit of slumping or collapsing your chest, use this visualization to provide a sense of ease and openness across your chest, releasing overworked neck and shoulder muscles.

- If you have the opposite pattern of lifting and thrusting your chest forward and up by pushing your heart against the breastbone, try releasing the weight of your heart into your hands and then exert slight pressure with your hands into your thighs. Feel the flow of energy move from your palms to your heart.

Sensory Focus

- Feel the contrast between energizing your hands to help support your heart or letting your hands play more of a passive role. Notice how these different intentions affect your body-mind and posture.

- Bring sensory awareness to the feeling of movement and flow from hand to heart, to opposite hand, and then back toward the heart. Feel the qualities of upliftedness, vitality, and fluid power as your hands gently support the suspension of the front of the chest and sternum.

Contemplation

- Our hands support our hearts and our hearts support our hands. As you go through your day, notice if your heart is behind your handshake or touch as you interact with others. Notice also if what and who you touch is brought back into your heart as feeling and connection.

If you find yourself feeling especially tight, spaced out, or disconnected when you begin a meditation session, it can be helpful to spend a few minutes simply breathing into your heart. Your breath is like a flashlight of awareness, illuminating what is held in your heart and reconnecting you to the tenderness of your feelings.

Breathe into the Heart

Intention: To feel how the heart helps support the chest and rib cage and to awaken the heart's natural vulnerability, gentleness, and compassion.

- To locate the general area of your heart, make a soft fist with your hand and place the top of your fist just below the level of your collarbone, slightly to the left of your breastbone. Your hand is considered roughly the size of your own heart, so the top of your fist will correspond to the top of your heart while your wrist will relate to the bottom of your heart.

- Once you have located this area, if it is comfortable, place your hand on your heart and tune in to your breathing.

- As you breathe, feel the movement of your lungs as they expand and release around your heart. With each breath, go deeper until your awareness rests in the subtle movement of the heart itself.

- Now visualize your breath moving into the four chambers of the heart. As you fill each "room" with breath, feel as if windows open in each chamber and let in fresh air, revitalizing and clearing away any stagnation.

- If you practice this for any length of time, you can begin to let the focus on your external breath begin to fade. You will become more aware of the liveliness of the heart tissue itself. The billions of cells that make up your heart are breathing, communicating with each other through their semipermeable membranes. This level of cellular awareness can bring a deep sense of relaxation and recuperation.

Sensory Focus

• Connect to the sense of uplift, vitality, and fluid power of the heart that can be felt to support the gentle suspension of the front of the chest and sternum.

• If you have a pattern of lifting and thrusting your chest forward and pushing your heart against the breastbone, try bringing awareness to the back of your heart. Awareness of the back surface of the heart softens the chest and brings a sense of rest and contentment.

• Allow feelings, emotions, or stories that arise out of your heart to simply be. If you stay with the circulation of the breathing, the feelings and emotions that bubble up will rise and then dissolve naturally.

Contemplation

• When we feel emotionally disconnected or unsynchronized, feeling our hearts can remind us to connect to how we actually feel. Take a moment to lightly breathe into your heart as you go about your day, noticing if you feel more synchronized with your feelings and emotions.

The organs are processing plants, communities of specialized cells that provide ongoing transformation. Food is turned into energy and heat; air transforms into life-giving oxygen for the cells and carbon dioxide for the natural world. As we tune in to these organs of transformation, we can feel qualities of emotional depth, richness, and uniqueness that enrich our meditation practice and physical presence.

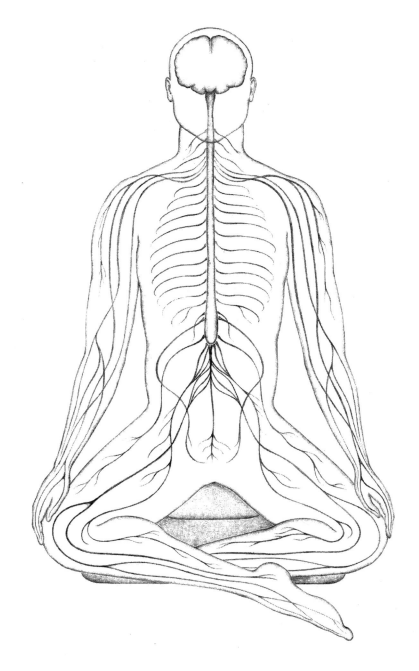

Figure 6: The Nervous System

8

Exquisite Sensitivity: Our Nerves

"Between stimulus and response, there is a space. In that space lies our freedom and power to choose our response. In our response lies our growth and freedom."

—Viktor Frankl

The nervous system is an exquisitely sensitive electrochemical feedback system designed to regulate, organize, and integrate the entire body-mind into a cohesive whole. Every change that occurs in the body-mind is registered through some aspect of the nervous system. Feeling our body, working with our posture, relating to our thought process and our emotions, engaging in the practice of mindfulness and awareness—all this occurs within the physiology and anatomy of the nervous system. It is the perceptual base from which we view and interact with our internal and external worlds.[47]

Sensing, Perceiving, and Responding

While extremely complex, the basic activity of the nervous system can be understood as a continual process of sensing, perceiving, and responding. We receive sensory information from the *peripheral nervous system*, which includes the sensory nerves embedded in skin, joints, viscera, bones, muscles, and sensory organs (eyes, ears, nose, and tongue). That information is relayed to the *central nervous system, spinal cord,* and *brain.* Based on these stimuli, perceptions are formed that involve modulating and comparing the incoming information with previous data, memory, and psychological projections or preconceptions. Based on our perception, a particular response takes place through the activation of the *motor nerves.* This can be referred to as the "sensory-motor loop."[48]

The act of perceiving and creating meaning can involve conscious choice, habitual response, or involuntary and unconscious response. Once perception has occurred, the motor nerves respond in accordance with our perception and intention to affect our inner or outer environment. The entire nervous system is essentially a continual dance between receptivity, meaning, and response. It is designed to maintain basic survival as well as continual growth and learning.

Linda Hartley states, "We actively perceive by shifting our attention toward certain stimuli and choosing which stimulation we will take in and register, consciously or unconsciously, in the process of organizing sensory information into recognizable and meaningful perceptions."[49] Actively focusing on particular stimuli is essential since we couldn't possibly integrate all the stimuli we receive moment to moment. Imagine that as you are reading this, you hear a loud bang. Your ears perk up and all your active attention is placed on listening. In that moment, you are both receiving sensory stimulation as well as actively forming a perception. In the next moment, you might respond by getting up and investigating to find out what's up. How you move, whether quickly and urgently or quietly and cautiously, is being informed by the continual feedback from your sensory nerves that are modulating your motor response.

In real time, this sensory-motor loop is exceedingly fast—especially when basic reflexes are engaged—in order to assure quick responses that relate to our very survival. If we can track this process cognitively, slowing it down enough to bring it into conscious awareness, we begin to notice our own relationship to receptivity and expression. Do we prefer to skip to the action before we've received clear information and feedback from our inner and outer environment? If we are not used to paying attention to the sensory information that we are receiving through all of our senses, it can be difficult to develop the clear perceptions that help us respond with appropriate action. We may find ourselves reacting habitually, repeating actions based on the well-worn pathways embedded in our nervous system. When we slow down enough to allow time to receive, process, and respond, our actions are more up to date, fresh, and uncontrived.

Meditation Practice and the Sensory-Motor Loop

Initially, it might appear that meditation practice and the posture of meditation cultivate more sensing and being than doing. Most mindfulness-awareness techniques emphasize learning to relax and stay present within the constant stream of incoming information from our nervous systems, neither blocking, elaborating, or trying to figure everything out. These tendencies are distractions from simply being present, based on our constant need to do something. In formal meditation, the body is positioned in a relatively still posture and the mind is encouraged to settle down. This can evoke a stark contrast to the rest of our lives, where there is an emphasis on doing and acting. Many of us feel we have little time for reflection, for listening to and feeling our own bodies and minds or the bodies and minds of those around us. The qualities of receptivity, openness, and quiet in meditation provide an essential antidote to the habitual busyness of our daily lives as we focus on "getting things done."

While it is true that the emphasis in meditation is less on action, the posture and practice of meditation together embody a subtler experience of the sensory-motor loop. We sit in stillness, sensing our body and the texture or quality of our mind, and yet we are not withdrawn—we are open, awake, and alert to our environment. In meditation, we can shift our awareness to an inner, sensory focus like feeling our body or breath, and to an outer, motor focus such as one-pointed attention on something. When we combine these qualities of both inner and outer focus through sensing, listening, perceiving, opening, and attentiveness, we are cultivating a balanced nervous system. As our meditation practice develops and we become more familiar and comfortable with simply being present, we begin to discover that our meditation practice has been training our perceptions to unfold into increasingly clear responses within our daily lives.

Below are a series of visualization practices to help you become more aware of the sensory/motor loop and its relationship to the sitting posture and meditation.[50]

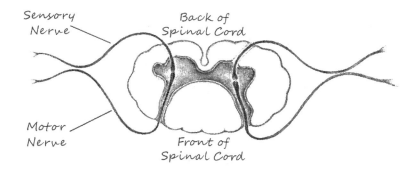

Figure 7: The Sensory-Motor Loop

Bring Awareness to the Sensory-Motor Loop

Intention: To increase body-mind integration and postural support by bringing equilibrium and awareness to the nervous system.

- Place your hands on your thighs and feel the sensations in your hands that are stimulated by touching your legs. Perhaps you feel heat, the texture of clothing—soft or rough, or the nerve endings in your skin tingling as you bring attention to your hands.

- Follow the sensations that occur along the network of sensory nerves, starting from your hands, moving up your arms, across your shoulders, and toward your upper back. Visualize the thread-like nerves entering the back of your spinal cord.[51] Keep increasing your awareness of the sensory nerves as more and more sensory information comes from your hands.

- Rest for a few moments in appreciation of the sensory nerves as clear pathways of communication, knowing that the sensations being communicated are as vital to your central nervous system as food and water. All sensation is basic nutrition for the nervous system, even pain. Without a constant flow of incoming messages from our inner and outer worlds, we would not survive.

- Bring your awareness to the place where the sensory nerves from your hands and arms enter the back of your spinal cord. You are entering the gateway to the central nervous system, the spinal cord. Rest here for a moment and allow any information that comes in to "do its thing."[52] In other words, trust your perceptions to unfold naturally, creating meaning as the information from the sensory nerves is relayed up and down the nerve tracts of the spinal cord to the various centers of the brain.

- Now bring your awareness to the front of your spinal cord and visualize the motor nerves branching out from your spinal cord to all areas of your body: your organs, muscles, and glands. If movement occurs as a response, allow it. As the motor nerves of your arms and hands are activated, you might feel the urge to open and spread your arms. Maybe your mouth responds by smiling, or your eyes light up, or you feel your heart energy radiate out. This is the motor phase, the natural desire to express, to communicate and engage.

- In this final phase, you can practice a more condensed version of the sensory-motor loop by simply shifting your perception to the front, back, and middle space of your body. First, feel the back of your spine, including the sense of space behind you. Then shift your attention to feel and rest in the central spinal cord, or wherever you perceive the middle layers of your body to be. Finally, shift your awareness to the front of your body and the front of your spine. Expand your awareness to include the space in front of your body. Finish your exploration by resting your awareness in your middle or center space, which can enhance your feeling of physical and psychological balance.

Sensory Focus

- Feel the natural, continual feedback loop that is occurring in your nervous system as you receive information, perceive, know what that information means, and respond to it.

- Feel the quality of your experience change as you shift from back, to the middle, to the front of your body. Can you feel a change from more inner focus to more outer focus as you shift through the layers of your body?

Contemplation

- When we are able to bring our awareness equally to all three phases of the nervous system—sensing, perceiving, and acting—we are repatterning deeply held habits of the body-mind. Fully sensing gives us the ability to feel more, physically and psychologically. Paying attention to the place in our physical body where meaning and perception are formed allows us to relax deeply and let go into simply being. Waking up the motor nerves enhances our presence as an engaged being. We are ready to make contact with our world; we are ready to touch others.[53]

Integrating Awareness of Your Nervous System into Your Meditation Practice

There are a number of ways that you can integrate the sensory-motor loop into your formal meditation practice. If your meditation practice involves focusing on your breath, allow the incoming breath to become a sensory experience: feel your body as the breath "moves" you. At the top of the in-breath, you might experience a gap of stillness (just don't confuse this with holding the breath), which touches into a sense of being and offers a moment of simple presence. As you breathe out, you open to the environment, subtly touching and engaging with your world as your breath mingles with the breath of all beings. At the end of an exhalation, you might experience another gap of presence before the in-breath reoccurs.

During your sitting practice, if you notice that you are feeling slightly numb or disconnected from your body, you can always imagine the pathways of sensation, the network of nerves as they enter into the back of your spine. If you find that you are feeling too introverted or disengaged from your environment, you can briefly visualize the motor nerves that radiate out the front of your spinal cord.

The Nervous System in Visual Perception

The eyes are, essentially, our brain exposed. They reflect our relationship to our nervous system[54] because how we perceive through the eyes exerts a strong influence on the balance of the nervous system altogether. There are a variety of traditional instructions on how to work with the eyes in the meditation practice, which are very specific because they support the particular goals of the practice.

When we close our eyes, we substantially reduce the amount of stimulation we take in and the amount of distraction we might experience. We naturally close our eyes as we drift toward sleep. If we want to remain awake and present, yet meditate with the eyes closed, our awareness will be more inwardly focused. With this inner focus, we are more easily able to access bodily sensations and emotional feelings. Visualizing might feel more accessible and vivid.

On the other hand, if our eyes remain wide open as we practice, all of our senses become more alert and engaged. Though we are not moving, our awareness is drawn outward. Because the eyes are such powerful perceptual organs, the focusing aspect of our motor nerves could make us feel restless as the visual stimulation of our environment draws us toward movement or action. We might suddenly notice dust in the corner that needs to be cleaned and have an urge to sweep it right away. For this reason, many meditation techniques work with the eyes partially closed, with the eyelids lowered. This strikes a balance between inner and outer focus.

Because the sense organs have both sensory and motor aspects, the eyes can receive information through their sensory nerves and they can focus directly on an object with the intent to see it with the motor nerves. A helpful way to navigate this in meditation practice is to maintain a "soft focus," an open gaze that does not focus directly on incoming visual information. This technique engages more of the sensory nerves of the eyes, releasing us from the habitual tendency to "motor" through the eyes in an attempt to secure ourselves though visual data.

Eye Gaze

Intention: To bring awareness to the role of the eyes in meditation and to understand the relationship of the eyes to the nervous system.

- At the beginning of your practice or when you are taking a relaxed walk, take a few moments to notice how you engage your eyes.

- First, soften your gaze so that you are not focusing on anything in particular. Allow the light and images in your environment to be received by the sensory nerves of your retina. Allow the visual information in without responding or commenting. Like a child or a newborn baby,[55] gaze at your world freshly and with a quality of open awareness.

- Then change your perception by engaging the motor nerves of your eyes and focusing your attention on a particular object or image that you see. Feel the precision and alertness of your focus and notice your response. Do you respond with a particular feeling or emotion? Do you think about or comment on what you are seeing? Is your curiosity piqued in some way?

- Continue to alternate your awareness between the sensory and motor nerves by first softening your gaze and then focusing your gaze. Then just relax and notice if by exercising both the sensory and motor nerves of the eyes you have found a natural balance between receiving and engaging your visual experience. Notice how this changes your state of mind. Can you feel a ground of visual receptivity and openness from which curiosity and discovery can arise?

Contemplation

- Since the eyes are the exposed part of the brain, become aware of the vulnerability in the eyes when communicating with others. Expressions like "Eyes are windows into the soul" and "Seeing eye-to-eye" express this natural intelligence. How do you engage your eyes in various spaces, situations, and relationships?

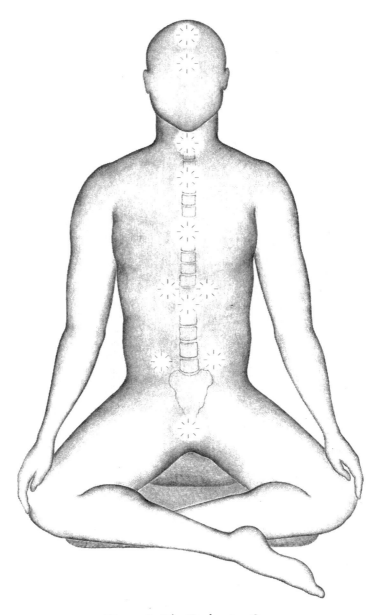

Figure 8: The Endocrine System
(from bottom to top: perineal and coccygeal body, gonads,
pancreas, adrenals, heart bodies, thymus, thyroid,
pituitary, mammillary—the pineal is not shown)

9

Energetic Essence:
Our Endocrine Glands

"Conscious use of the endocrine system can help us create a clearer and more integrated alignment of the physical body, and of the body with the mind, and feelings that are expressed through it."

—Linda Hartley

In the posture of meditation, the endocrine glands provide a delicate, yet powerful, energetic support for the entire body. An endocrine gland is any organ that produces a chemical secretion, called a *hormone*, directly into the bloodstream. Through a feedback system of inhibition or stimulation, these chemicals regulate the activities of all the cells in the body, providing constant balance and homeostasis to an organism that is in constant flux in response to the body's internal and external environment. This happens in dialogue with the central nervous system[56] as it responds to the hormonal surges in a continual feedback loop, triggering the individual glands to greater or lesser activity.

The glandular system is linked to the more ancient parts of our brain and the "involuntary" or autonomic nervous system. The functions of the autonomic system are more primal and fundamental than the relatively modern cerebral cortex, as they include our basic sense of survival. Hormones such as adrenalin and cortisol that are released in response to threatening situations (the fight-or-flight responses)[57] are part of the sympathetic nervous system. Hormones that are part of the parasympathetic nervous system modulate and inhibit these hormonal surges and stimulate hormones that bring us into a more relaxed and calm state.

When we visualize, breathe, touch, or send sound into the glands, we are tapping into a natural "inner pharmacy." Because the glands release their hormones directly into the bloodstream, the result is a wide range of emotional and body-mind states.[58] By taking the posture of meditation and resting in stillness, with light awareness on the glands, our autonomic functions of basic survival feel nourished. We are honoring the "automatic" part of the autonomic nervous system—the ability of our body-mind to find balance emotionally, psychologically, and spiritually—through the complex interrelationship of our chemical, electrical, and energetic systems.

While all the tissues of the body have an energetic charge, the glands in particular vibrate at a higher frequency than other tissues. In the sitting posture, when the network of glands are stimulated along the front of the spine, they bring lightness and an energetic radiance that appears to extend beyond the physical body. For this reason, some have likened the endocrine glands to the ancient yogic system of the chakras and the energetic channels of traditional Chinese medicine. According to Linda Hartley, "The endocrine glands have been described as being one of the subtlest manifestations of energy in the physical body, related closely to the chakras. They could be seen as a link between the subtle and invisible energy body and the manifest physical body."[59] This is an emerging inquiry that is beyond the scope of this book, but I also encourage you to make your own connections to traditional energetic systems and the endocrine system through direct somatic inquiry.[60] What perceptual, emotional, and physical changes do you experience when you contact the specific glands? Is there a resonance between the specific glands and energy centers you are familiar with?

In a developing infant, the glands are first stimulated into action through the stress of gravity. As the infant begins the journey toward verticality, gravity exerts a powerful force along the whole length of the spine, affecting the individual glands that are primarily lined up along the central axis of the spine. As the glands are stimulated, they lend lightness and energetic support to potential areas of weakness or collapse.[61] For example, when a baby is on her belly and wants to lift her head to see her mother, glands are stimulated in the area of the upper chest and neck to lend energetic support to a movement that goes against the downward pull of gravity. In the same way, when you take the posture of meditation, you can tap into glandular support all along the front of the spine for more effortless verticality and energetic support for your entire structure.

For the purposes of working with the posture of meditation, we will focus on a number of key glands and glandular tissues[62] as explored through the somatic techniques of Body-Mind Centering. By placing your awareness on these glands, you will find a gateway to the experience of energy as it moves through your body and beyond your body, affecting and intermingling with your environment.

Grounding with the Lower Glands

Meditation and somatic teachers often emphasize grounding ourselves and our energy. Chögyam Trungpa would tell his students that when we do not physically and psychologically relate to our earthy experience, we tend to float above, or perch on, our meditation cushion.[63] In many traditions, the embodiment of this grounding energy is found in the center of the pelvic floor and at the very base of the spine. The *perineal body*[64] is located in the very center of the perineum where the muscles and fascia that make up the pelvic diaphragm converge. It is the point between the sitz bones and the anal sphincters and either the vaginal sphincter or base of the penis. The *coccygeal body* is a small mass of endocrine tissue located at the tip of the tailbone.[65] While these two glands root and ground us, they also bring lightness and power to our seat, offering a counterpoint to the weighted quality we might feel when we relax our lower organs and release into the weight of our bones.[66] On either side of the body, midway between the navel and the pubic bone, are the reflex points for the *gonads* or sex glands. While these are the locations for the ovaries in women, for men, these reflex points are located along the top of the loop of the vas deferens tube, the area from which the testes originally descended to the scrotum.

Energetically, the perineal body and coccygeal body ground the head glands so that, like a balloon with a tether, our higher visionary centers remain connected to the earth and to the "real world." The gonads ground us physically by supporting the alignment of our pelvic halves, sacrum, lower legs, and ankles. Energetically, the gonads have a connection with the throat or thyroid gland; both are centers of expression, creativity, and communication.

Connecting the Lower and Upper Body through the Middle Glands

The *adrenal glands* sit directly on top of the kidneys and connect to the navel center. The adrenal glands, like the kidneys, connect the lower body to the upper body and provide energetic support at the lumbar curve, a vulnerable area of the spine. In the section on the organs, we brought awareness to the kidneys in order to release lower-back tension and allow movement and energy to flow through an area where we tend to chronically hold tension. Working with the adrenals adds another layer of support, as they are more energetic in nature than the kidneys and are directly connected to stress and anxiety responses.

The *pancreas* is both a gland and an organ that is situated right below the respiratory diaphragm in the area of the solar plexus. Because of its central location in the middle of the body, in front of the kidneys and behind the stomach and liver, the pancreas radiates its energy to all the limbs of the body like the spokes of a wheel, lightening and energizing our entire body.[67]

As we move our awareness up the front of the spine, the qualities of our body-mind shift from rootedness and earthiness to expansion and engagement. We experience width and breadth as we move from deep, primal energy to more fully engage with our world. In this respect, the glands located near our solar plexus can be considered glands of transformation from rootedness to expansion and openness.

Expanding and Opening with the Upper Glands

The *heart bodies* are located behind the middle of the sternum and are the glandular energy centers of the heart organ.[68] In the organ chapter we discussed the cross-cultural power that the metaphor and experience of the heart has for human beings. As Dr. Mimi Guarneri says in *The Heart Speaks*, if we are asked to touch where we feel love, we probably won't reach for the stomach or the brain.[69] When we fall in love and think of our beloved, we can feel a surge of warmth and energy in the area near our heart. When we confront the suffering of others, we feel it physically in the heart as sensitive tenderness or heavy sadness. The difference between the heart as an organ and as a gland is subtle. The organ heart gives a sense of volume, width, and soft power to the upper body, while the energy of the glandular heart extends beyond the body. There is a natural quality of opening without needing to push our energy outward or thrust our ribs and heart forward.

The *thymus*, a gland connected to our immune system and the natural defense of the body, is located directly behind the upper part of the sternum or breastbone. The thymus supports a widening and opening across the shoulders and with that posture, a sense of bravery and courage. This upper part of the chest is where you would "pin your medals" on your uniform, expressing a kind of fierce dignity.

The *thyroid* is a gland located just below the thyroid cartilage, the Adam's apple. It's reflex point, which is where we can touch the gland to stimulate or make contact with it, is in the front and center of the thyroid cartilage. It is directly connected with our voice, and is a strong center of communication, creativity, and engagement. Bonnie says, "When you find the thyroid, all the glands can perk up ... something lights up. The thyroid governs cellular metabolism. When it comes into awareness, all the cells resonate."[70] In this way, the thyroid opens up all the energy centers along the spine and also supports the head. It is a key gland to bring into balance so that our head is properly aligned, skeletally and energetically.

Suspending with the Head Glands

There are three head glands located in the brain: the *pituitary*, the *mammillary bodies*, and the *pineal*. These glands are all situated on an imaginary diagonal line through the skull, traced from the bridge of the nose back through the center of the brain and out the birthing crown slightly to the back of the head. If you breathe in through your nose and follow this upward diagonal line toward the back of your skull through the center of your brain, from front to back you are stimulating the pituitary, the mammillary bodies, and the pineal gland.[71]

The mammillary bodies, located in the center of the brain, are a keystone to the whole neuroendocrine system and a pivot point between the front and back of the body. The central axis of our spine is directly supported by the mammillary bodies and the energy of this gland extends out the top of the head to the "heavens" and beyond. The mammillary bodies help bring us into the fullness of the present moment.

The pituitary gland supports the eyes, connecting us to inner and outer vision as well as a sense of expanding our awareness forward in time and space. And the pineal gland has a quality of reaching back in time. With the pineal gland, there is a natural cycling back to our lower glands, to our rootedness, to earth.

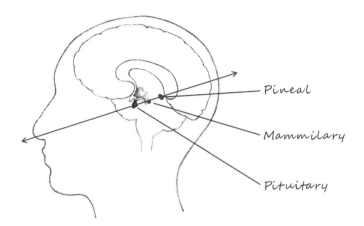

Figure 9: Breathing into the Head Glands

Making Contact with the Glands

Because the functions of the glands are always in relationship to each other,[72] forming an interdependent chain along the front of the spine, it is important to be delicate and gentle as you connect with the glands. Over-stimulating any one gland will affect all the other glands in the chain.

Because the energy fields of the glands and the chakras extend well beyond the physical body, and because sound vibrations also travel beyond the physical body, sound is a potent technique for awakening glandular and energetic activity. Using your own voice to sound into particular glands in order to stimulate and feel them, is particularly powerful because of the subtle, vibratory quality of endocrine tissue. Once you have located these glands experientially, you might find that certain kinds of music stimulate these different centers. For example, the clear, high-pitched, crystalline sound of Gregorian chants can open up our head glands, and the deep, low-pitched sound of Tibetan horns and overtone chanting resonates in our lower glands. It is also important to trust where you actually feel an energetic connection in terms of the actual locations of glandular tissue and/or chakras. While the location of the glands doesn't vary between individuals, the exact area where one feels an energetic charge can vary.

Bones, muscles, and organs provide us with feelings of substance and structure—bringing awareness to the glands supports the experience of wholeness in the body-mind and energizes our entire being.

Turn on the Glands

Intention: To bring the glandular energy centers along the spine into balance and increase the flow of energy through the body for effortless and supported posture.

- Sitting or lying down, bring your awareness to your pelvic floor, the area between your sitz bones, tail, and pubic bone. Visualize a bundle of glandular tissue, like a little knob at the center of the pelvic floor where the perineal body is located. Breathe into the area and visualize light extending out. "Turn on" this gland by imagining that you are slowly turning on a light that is on a dimmer switch. As you turn up the light, feel the illumination spread through your body, especially your legs, feet, and pelvis.

- Next, move your awareness to the tip of your tail and turn on the "dimmer switch" of your coccygeal body, again diffusing the light through your lower body.

- Now feel the energy of your gonads, located approximately two inches from your midline between your navel and pubis on either side. Let your light bathe your sacrum and pelvis as it radiates internally. You can then extend that radiation beyond your physical body, into the surrounding space.

- Move your awareness up your spine to the adrenal glands, which are located on top of the kidneys in the lumbar curve of your spine, behind your navel. As you visualize light in this center, imagine it emanating like spokes of a wheel that extend to the entire periphery of your body.

- Now feel the pancreas in the solar plexus area, located under the sternum and diaphragm. Allow the image and feeling of light to extend out beyond your pancreas to your head, hands, feet and tail.

- Feel your heart center behind the middle of your breastbone and radiate light from your heart bodies, which illuminate from inside your shoulders, chest, arms, and hands. The heart is an area that vibrates with feelings. As you light up that area, notice your emotional responses to energizing the heart bodies.

- From your heart, shift your awareness to your thymus, in the upper part of your sternum. Like your heart, this can be an emotional area and it also contains a powerful and palpable sense of radiating outward and suspending upward.

- Move up to your throat and sense the area behind your thyroid cartilage or Adam's apple. This is the energy center for the thyroid gland. As you use your dimmer switch to light up your throat and illuminate your head and shoulder area, you might feel a further brightness that touches all the glands.

- For the head glands, bring your awareness up through your neck and brainstem and back toward your pineal gland. Feeling this sweep up the back will give energetic support to the back of the skull. Extend light out the back of the skull, opening that area to sensation. Move your awareness forward on a slight downward diagonal and find the pituitary in the brain just behind the eyebrows. Send light out from this center, counterbalancing the energy from the pineal in the back. The light fills your eyes and opens up your vision as you look out and forward. Now bring awareness to the mammillary bodies, right in the center of the brain and feel that area as a center point between the pineal and the pituitary.

- As light extends out the top of your head from this point, let your awareness move all the way down the chain of glands to the perineal body, connecting through an open channel from the very bottom of your spine to the top. Rest in open awareness of light intermingling and permeating all your centers. Feel the vibratory nature of glandular energy as it both moves within your body and radiates out beyond your physical body.

Sensory Focus

- As you make contact with the glands, feel their energies move in an interconnected chain up and down your spine. This is one of the reasons yoga and other somatic practices emphasize movement and awareness of the spine. Like a string of brightly colored Christmas lights, as the glands "light up," a current is carried along from bulb to bulb. The guided imagery emphasizes gently "turning the glands on" and allowing the energy to move through the whole body. Glandular energy feels clear, direct, and crystalline.

- Remember that you control the dimmer switch. The brighter the light you generate, the more stimulation to that area. Be gentle and don't push, as even a little bit of focus on the glands can be quite powerful. It is fine to keep the light low or to bring it down whenever it feels even a little bit overwhelming, especially if you are not used to feeling energy move in the body.

Contemplation

- Because the glands are linked to the autonomic nervous system, which controls homeostasis and through the release of hormones elicits primal emotional responses, we can have a direct experience of psychophysical balance or imbalance by focusing on this system. Questions that you ask yourself might include:

o Does my body-mind feel more energized when I focus on the endocrine system?

o Do I feel more calm and relaxed?

o Do I notice areas of imbalance or stress?

o Can I notice the emotional qualities of the different glands?

10

Going with the Flow: Our Fluids

"The primary characteristic of any fluid system is its ability to keep transforming itself."

—Emilie Conrad

Between 50 to 80 percent of our body's tissues are fluid-based—depending on our age, gender, and to some degree our fluid intake. The percentage of water on the surface of the Earth is calculated at about 71 percent, reflecting our own body composition. Linda Hartley beautifully states the relationship of our body's fluid nature with the body of the Earth:

> Within the body we find expressions of all the forms in which water circulates on, in, and around the Earth. In us there is the great un-bounded ocean of fluid in which all the cells are bathed. There are rivers and streams flowing within the vessels of the veins, arteries, lymphatic, and cerebrospinal fluid channels; there are pools and reservoirs and places where the fluid gushes or trickles like springs, waterfalls, or rain. There may also be places where the flow is blocked and the fluid stagnates.[73]

When we resonate with our fluid nature, we feel more relaxed, at ease, and flexible. We are reminded that we are less solid than we perceive ourselves to be. In some sense, we are made up of only one fluid—primarily water—that is in a constant state of transformation as it flows through different channels and picks up different molecules and substances.[74] The ability of fluids to transform, cleanse, lubricate, circulate information, and connect all parts of us into a whole inspires powerful metaphors for a healthy sense of our own body-mind as being on a continuum and in a constant state of flow.

In the meditation posture, healthy circulation of our bodily fluids is reflected in the ease of our breathing, the levels of tension or tone in our musculature, and the emotional feeling we allow ourselves to experience. When we breathe shallowly or "hold" the breath, there is less oxygen being delivered through the flow of our fluids, and when muscles are habitually contracted, there will be less circulation to that area. When we feel ourselves emotionally stuck, we can feel our fluids damming up. We've all felt the sense of release through fluids such as tears, laughter, and sweat when we are feeling strong emotions or simply moving the body vigorously.

Four traditional Buddhist analogies for meditative experiences are inspired by fluid: our meditations can be likened to a waterfall, a rushing brook, a slowly flowing stream, or a still pool.[75] We can recognize these fluid images as states of body-mind on a continuum, from the waterfall and tumbling of our thought process to the calm abiding we experience as our thoughts settle down. These meditative experiences express the very different ways our body-mind is in a constant process of flux and change. We can use this potent imagery of the fluids to support deep relaxation and ease in the meditation posture. Fluids that are especially supportive to the practice and posture of meditation are found within the cells, in the ocean the cells are bathed in (the intracellular and extracellular fluids), and in the fluid that nourishes and lubricates the brain and spinal cord.

Cellular and Intercellular Fluid

Approximately two-thirds of the fluids in the body are within the cellular membranes. With the imagery of our fluid-filled cells, we return to a primordial sense of being—to our original experience as a one-celled creature, a semipermeable membrane filled with fluid. This is how life itself began and where we return to touch the quiet pool of our origin. Bonnie describes the experience of cellular fluid as "the state of absolute rest and moment-by-moment presence, with nothing to do and nowhere to go."[76] The *intercellular fluid*, which is the fluid matrix surrounding all our cells, is the connective tissue that binds and brings every part of our body into communication with every other part. It is our inner ocean: flowing, moving, and expressing all the qualities of oceanic power.

Fluid Ground

Intention: To experience the restful quality of the fluid within the cells as well as the subtle flow and inner waves of movement of the fluid around the cells.

- To connect with the deep rest and recuperation that bringing awareness to your cellular fluid brings, you might want to first lie down so that you can feel the weightiness and release of your "fluid pools." The guided exercises "Yielding" and "Cellular Breathing" offered in other chapters can remind you to connect with your supporting surface so you can fully let go into gravity.

- Once you feel supported, imagine all the billions of cells in your body (or just a few) as quiet, still ponds, remembering that water has weight and that it can settle.

- Shift your awareness to an area of tension in your body. This could be muscular tension or a feeling of holding in any of your organs. Close your eyes and visualize that area as soft tissue made up of millions of cells that are swimming in an ocean of fluid.

- Visualize that the fluid moves the cells and the cells move the fluid in a mutual exchange. Let yourself identify with the subtle movement of both the fluid within the cells as well as the movement of the cells in the fluid ocean.

- When you are ready, add the feeling and visualization of your breath as it affects pressure changes in the fluid. Feel, as you inhale, that the fluid is drawn in one direction. As you exhale, it is moved along in another direction. Your breath makes waves in the fluids and it has a ripple effect through the tissues. It is like the tide coming in and going out; the pressure changes that occur through breathing help move the fluids through the body.

- Begin to move and stretch, feeling how your inner ocean connects all the tissues of the body. Gently contract your toes, sending fluid up your leg and toward your core. Like squeezing a tube of toothpaste or a gel pack, wherever we knead or squeeze our tissues, fluids are moved through the whole body.

Contemplation

• During a meditation session, tuning in to your "fluid pools" or the "inner ocean" of fluids can bring deep recuperation, subtle flow, and softness to your posture—especially when you feel tight or frozen. As you go through your day, resonate with the bodies of water around you. Notice the droplets of water on your kitchen counter, in your bath water, swimming pool, or the ocean, their perfect spheres each making a whole. As evolutionary beings, we never left the ocean; we hold it within us.

Cerebrospinal Fluid

The *cerebrospinal fluid (CSF)* is produced in spaces of the brain called *ventricles*. It is a clear fluid that envelops and cushions the brain, draining downward and surrounding the spinal cord with a fluid shock-absorber. So that there is little gravitational force, or pull, on this central axis, the brain and spinal cord are literally floating in fluid. In a feedback system, the CSF is first produced in the ventricles of the brain (the filling stage). The CSF then drains downward, bathing the spinal cord (the emptying stage). As the fluid drains, the ventricles are stimulated to produce more CSF and the filling and emptying stages continue. This pressure buildup and release can be felt in the tissues of the body as a subtle rhythm. It is this quality and rhythm of movement that is the focus of some osteopathic and craniosacral therapy techniques.[77]

According to Bonnie Cohen, "The cerebrospinal fluid relates to meditative rest and the central core of unbounded self."[78] Qualities we might experience when we bring awareness to this fluid are a sense of timelessness, sustained flow and lightness, deep rest and recuperation, and a balancing of our nervous system. The fluid-filled spaces, or ventricles, in the brain lend a sense of lightness to our skull and the bathing of our spinal cord in fluid brings soft, suspended movement to our central axis. It is possible to notice this subtle CSF rhythm of filling and emptying when we are settled and relaxed in a meditation session. We might become aware of a subtle rhythm underneath the movement of inhaling and exhaling that seems to travel from the brain, down the central channel or spinal cord. The rhythm of the CSF is slower than the breath, taking between two or three breaths to complete a cycle of filling and emptying.

To sense the cerebrospinal fluid, settle into your meditation practice for a few minutes. If you have been focusing on the rhythm and feeling of your external breathing, at some point, let that focus go. Bring your awareness to your brain and spinal cord and notice if you can feel the CSF rhythm underneath the breath. Even if you are not sure what you are feeling, just imagine following the flow; imagining the ventricles filling with clear fluid and then draining and lubricating in and around the central axis of the spinal cord.

You might also choose to visualize some of the clear CSF fluid following along the pathways of the nerves as they branch out of the spine to your limbs and all parts of your body. Can you visualize your spinal cord and brain lightly suspended in fluid? Does this quality of suspension and nourishment to your nervous system relieve excess tension in your shoulders and neck? Notice the quality of your mind.

Water is soft power—it has the ability to effect deep change, to cleanse and renew, to dissolve any habit we may have of experiencing our bodies and minds as solid and unchangeable. As you go through your day, find moments to resonate with the qualities of water. When you see water, visualize your inner fluids moving, transforming, and cleansing the toxins from your body. When you touch water, feel its power and softness, and identify those qualities as your own. When you hear water, know that the rush of fluids through your body also has sound and vibration.

The fluids in the body are constantly undergoing change and transformation. Resonating and identifying with our innate fluidity supports our ability to transform our being in each moment, to let go, and flow forward with ease.

11

The Life Force: Our Breath

"The breathing soothes the mind and it allows it to rest. As our thoughts slow down and we settle into ourselves, the division between mind and body lessens."

—Sakyong Mipham

Traditionally, the breath has been praised as a particularly well-suited object of meditation. It is also a focal point for many contemporary mindfulness-based practices.[79] Feeling our breath links us directly to the felt sense of the body. Focusing on the breath is one of the most potent ways to receive feedback from all the tissues of the body: the more we consciously breathe into the body's tissues, the more feeling and awareness we have of those tissues and their "mind." As we breathe out, our breath dissolves into the atmosphere and we are brought into relationship with the natural world. In this way, through the breath our inner and outer worlds are joined and the seeming boundary between those worlds is softened. The breathing process expresses the natural balance between taking in what is needed to sustain our life force and letting go of what is not needed. Our respiratory process is the epitome of discernment and wisdom; it embodies the ability to separate what is life-giving and supportive from what is potentially harmful.

The Relationship of External Breath to the Internal Breathing Process

In the section on the lungs, we brought awareness to external respiration by following the breath as it entered our mouth and nostrils, moved down through our breathing tube and into the lobes of the lungs, and then released from our body as our lungs emptied. In the following section on the diaphragms, we will discuss the relationship of the thoracic diaphragm and the pelvic diaphragm to the breathing process. But there is another, internal breathing process that is occurring simultaneously.

After each inhalation, the breath enters the spongy tissue of the lungs; oxygen is transported through the circulatory system and eventually distributed throughout the whole body via the fluid surrounding the cells. At this point, the breath "rides on fluid" as the oxygen molecules, carried by the intercellular fluid, flow through a cell's semiporous membrane. Carbon dioxide then flows out of the cell into the surrounding fluid, entering the capillaries, veins, and lungs, and is eventually released into the atmosphere. This process of the cellular exchange of oxygen and carbon dioxide is called "internal respiration" or "cellular breathing."

Awareness of this subtle movement of breath at the cellular level makes us feel alive, whole, and present. The ability of all the cells to fully breathe is a baseline of health and well-being. When we feel emotional distress, physical pain, or unease, fear can numb parts of our body as we attempt to "wall off" sensation or feeling. By unconsciously rejecting parts of our self, we can unwittingly decrease the flow of oxygen to our tissues. As a result, we might experience excess tension, pain, or dullness in these areas.

Cellular Breathing Is Whole-Body Breathing

When we meditate, we have the opportunity to bring cellular awareness to the whole body by practicing whole-body breathing. "Allowing" is the keyword to doing this; we are not attempting to breathe more deeply or expend any special effort to pull the breath into the lungs or overwork the diaphragm.[80] The body remains in a state of openness and receptivity so that breath just happens.

When the focus of our meditation is the breath, we can allow a sense of spreading or rippling to occur through the body as our breath becomes fluid and moves into the cells. As we breathe out, we can feel a further softening and letting go of resistance at the cellular membranes. In the natural gap between our external inhalation and exhalation, there can be a sense of whole-body inspiration as all of our cells receive nourishment. In the gap following our exhalation, we can invite a sense of total release and a softening of our cellular membranes as we let go of the breath.

Whatever our object of meditation, sometimes letting go of focusing on the rhythm of the external breathing and turning attention instead to the subtle quality of cellular presence[81] or subtle cellular breathing will enliven and energize our practice, leading us into deeper experiences of stillness and presence.

"Change Is Just a Membrane Away"

When Bonnie Bainbridge Cohen's students are confronted with stubborn, deep-seated, psychophysical patterns of response, she encourages them by offering the reminder that "change is just a membrane away." By this she means that change—experienced in the differentiation between what to accept and what to reject, as well as the basic wisdom of decision-making—happens at the cellular level. The cell's semiporous membrane must "decide" what to let in and what to keep out, what will bring nourishment and what will bring harm. If there is confusion at this level, dis-ease can be its result. Awareness of cellular breathing brings us to that moment of discriminating intelligence.

To integrate cellular breathing more fully into your meditation practice, it is helpful to first practice cellular breathing off of your meditation cushion, either lying down or before falling asleep. You can guide yourself into a general awareness of whole-body breathing or you can focus on a specific area of your body that is experiencing stress or pain. It can be quite miraculous to experience the relief and release we can feel in any part of our body when we focus directly on an awareness of the breathing process of our cells.

Cellular Breathing

Intention: To cultivate whole-body breathing, which enhances embodiment and relaxes and enlivens our body-mind.

- In a comfortable and restful posture, bring awareness to your external breathing. Feel the coolness of the breath as it enters your nose and mouth. Feel the expansion of your breathing tube, the *trachea*, along the front of your throat as you follow the breath down into your gently expanding lungs. Notice the moment when your breath seems to be suspended, and then the slow release and softening of the lungs as the breath is released. Settle into this for a while.

- At some point, let go of focusing on the inhalation and exhalation. Place your hands on a sensitive or distressed area of your body, or simply bring your awareness to the sensations in that area. Taking your time, feel whatever you feel. Then bring an image or a feeling to mind of living, breathing tissue made up of hundreds of millions of cells. You might visualize just one cell or many cells.

- Imagine the flexible, semiporous membrane of the cell subtly opening to receive the fluid that carries oxygen, the breath of life. Then visualize the cellular membrane opening again, allowing carbon dioxide to flow out.

Sensory Focus

- As you work with the imagery, you might feel a subtle pulsing in the tissue as each cell expands and condenses in the breathing process. You might also notice a feeling of heat or tingling, or a sensation of deep rest and contentment. As pleasant as these sensations might feel, one can also become aware of a feeling of constriction and the difficulty of breathing fully into this area. You might feel numb or empty. You might feel the painful stirring of energy as that area awakens, not unlike anesthesia wearing off after surgery. Whatever you feel, accept that you are experiencing your vital life force, cell by cell and breath by breath.

Contemplation

- At the cellular level, the breathing process expresses the natural balance between taking in what is needed to sustain our life force and letting go of what is not needed. Our entire respiratory process expresses discernment and wisdom; it embodies the ability to separate what is life-giving and supportive from what is potentially harmful.

Engaging the Muscular Diaphragms for Support

The tone and action of the main diaphragms in the body support our core and bring strength to the sitting posture. The main diaphragms to focus on are the *thoracic* diaphragm and the *pelvic* diaphragm.[82] Both of these muscular structures have very particular roles to play in our basic survival. The respiratory, or thoracic diaphragm, is essential to the breathing process. The pelvic diaphragm, or pelvic floor, acts along with the thoracic to create pressure in the body for coughing, giving birth, defecating, and sexual activity.

The word *diaphragm*[83] comes from the Greek word meaning "a partition or wall; a divider." Diaphragms are muscular structures that provide a tensile, horizontal support to the majority of muscle fibers and connective tissue in the body that are running longitudinally. Diaphragms are transverse dividers, running from back to front and side to side as opposed to up and down in the body. Because of the diaphragm's horizontal orientation, these structures add support to our verticality by distributing the downward gravitational pull away from the central axis, into the horizontal plane.[84] Just like a spinning top is able to balance around its vertical axis because part of its structure is in the horizontal plane, the diaphragm offers support to the rest of the muscles in the body by helping to distribute the workload more efficiently.

The Thoracic Diaphragm

The thoracic diaphragm is considered the main muscle of breathing; without it we cannot bring air into our lungs and subsequently into our cells. The diaphragm, a powerful sheath of muscle, is attached in the back, to the front of the spine, the lower ribs, and the breastbone in front. Sometimes referred to as the *thoracic floor*, it divides the upper body from the lower body. The central tendon, or *crura*, of the diaphragm is anchored to the front of the spine at about the same level of the breastbone in front. This central tendon connects all the way down along the front of the spine, with some of its fibers blending into the pelvic floor.[85]

This shows the intimate relationship between the breathing process, the thoracic diaphragm, the spine, and the pelvic floor.[86] If we tend to lock or tighten our back muscles to try to conform to a particular posture, we might be impeding the fullness of the breath because the diaphragm is restricted. In the same way, if we restrict the movement of the diaphragm by holding our breath, we are also impacting the natural wave-like movements that occur in the spine as we breathe.

The heart and lungs rest on the top surface of the diaphragm and all the other major organs are tucked underneath the diaphragm muscles' two dome-like structures, which create an airtight barrier. When we inhale, the diaphragm widens and spreads, pulling the lungs and ribs outward and slightly downward, creating a vacuum that air rushes in to fill. While the downward movement of the diaphragm increases the compression of the lower digestive organs, it expands the space that the lungs can fill. As carbon dioxide builds up in the body, the brain signals the diaphragm to release upwards, decreasing the pressure on the lower organs and once again, increasing compression on the lungs. As we exhale, the air pressure inside the lungs is equalized with the air pressure outside our bodies and the cycle begins again.

This diaphragmatic pressure against the lower and upper organs as it moves up and down gently massages the organs, increasing their tone, circulation, and function. Even the shape of the heart changes as it rides on top of the diaphragm, from slightly elongated to more square from being pulled downward and upward. Activating the full movement of the diaphragm, which is sometimes referred to as "diaphragmatic breathing" or "belly breathing," has been shown to have a profound effect on reducing stress levels and anxiety. It is easy to see how restrictions related to the breathing process affect the health and well-being of our entire body and mind.

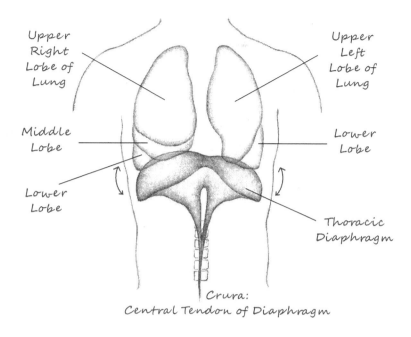

Figure 10: Activating the Thoracic Diaphragm

Activate Your Thoracic Diaphragm

Intention: To locate and activate the thoracic diaphragm for efficient breathing and upper-body support in the meditation posture.

- To locate the thoracic diaphragm, place your hands around your lower-to-middle ribs and cough. You should be able to feel the muscle of the diaphragm engaging (along with the *intercostal muscles*, which are small muscles between the ribs) and creating pressure to activate the cough.

- Having located the diaphragm, breathe and focus on the movement of the diaphragm underneath your hands. You might find that you have more movement of the diaphragm in the front part of the ribs and breastbone than you do around the sides and into the back of the ribs, where the diaphragm is also attached. If so, focus on initiating your diaphragmatic breathing in the lower back and side ribs.

- The diaphragm has been compared to a parachute that balloons upward as you exhale and as you inhale, it is pulled downward, its domes flattening. How much vertical movement up and down the spine can you feel as you inhale and exhale? How much horizontal movement can you feel as the bottom and sides of your ribs expand outward on the inhalation and release back on the exhalation?

- As you breathe, experience how the diaphragm moves the organs. Your lower organs move slightly outward as the diaphragm presses down on them and your lungs fill and expand.

- To bring awareness to the movement and support of your diaphragm in the sitting posture, take a few deep breaths to engage the diaphragm fully and then feel it gently pressing down and then slowly releasing upward. Keep your shoulder and neck muscles relaxed, feeling as if they are just going along for the ride—not tightening or trying to do the work of the diaphragm. If you make a hissing sound as you breathe out, this will increase the length of your exhalation and the feeling of your diaphragm slowly releasing upward along the front of your spine.

- Now shift your attention to taking smaller breaths. Maintain awareness of the subtle movement of the diaphragm in its upward and downward motion, as well as the sensation of widening in the lower ribs as they expand with the breath.

Sensory Focus

- Practice letting your breath become more and more subtle while keeping the sensation of support and width that comes from visualizing the diaphragm as a surface or platform that divides the upper and lower body and supports the heart, lungs, and shoulder girdle from below. Sense how your arms and shoulders can rest on the supportive platform of your diaphragm, which allows tight shoulder and neck muscles to release.

Contemplation

- Reflect on how the movement, or lack of movement, in your diaphragm mirrors the state of your body-mind as you go through your day and as you practice meditation. Notice if you find yourself holding your breath as you perform various activities and become curious about why that might be so. Do you notice a lack of movement in your diaphragm when you feel anxious? When you feel even slightly threatened, does your diaphragm feel like it's pulling up rather than spreading downward as you take a breath?

The Pelvic Diaphragm

The *pelvic diaphragm*, also referred to as the "perineum" or "pelvic floor," is the muscular area between your two sitz bones, your pubic bone, and your tailbone. If you trace an imaginary line along the periphery between those boney landmarks that make up the bottom of the pelvic bowl, you will have a diamond shape with four distinct quadrants that relate to specific muscles that make up the pelvic floor. Toward the center of the perineum, there is the anal sphincter and either the vaginal sphincter or root of the penis. All of the fibers of the perineum converge at these sphincters, as well as at the center of the diamond. Within this central area is the *perineal body* referred to in the section on the glands. In previous chapters, we have discussed how the pelvis provides our base of support, especially in the sitting posture. The perineum is the powerful muscular sling that supports our lower organs and provides vitality, and depth to the breath.

To sense the energy and power of this area, as well as the connection of the pelvic floor to our emotions and psychology, observe your pet dog's tail. The muscles that move that tail are the muscles of the pelvic diaphragm. A happy dog lifts its tail, wagging joyously at his master's return; a scared or aggressive dog tucks its tail under between its legs. A dog person will tell you too that there are many other signals of communication reflected in the movement of a dog's tail. While our own tails might not be as overtly expressive as Fido's, the support our pelvic diaphragm can provide in all our daily activities, including the sitting posture of meditation, is underrated. We rarely experience the full potentiality of the pelvic floor except for defecating and lovemaking—important activities to be sure, but limited in terms of the energy, power, and support our pelvic diaphragm can provide.

When we activate the pelvic floor, the support and tone we feel expresses itself through our whole body. When we connect the pelvic floor to our breathing, there is a natural deepening and aliveness that moves through our groin and down through our legs.

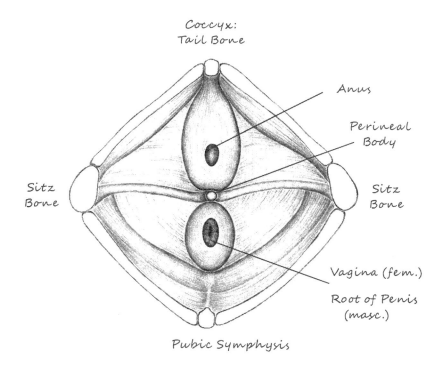

Figure 11: The Pelvic Diaphragm

Engage Your Pelvic Diaphragm

Intention: To engage the support of the pelvic diaphragm in the sitting posture.

- Sit on your meditation cushion or chair and find the boney landmarks that describe the perimeter of the diamond shape of the pelvic diaphragm. You can do this by rocking side to side to find the sitz bones and rocking forward and backward between your pubic bone and tail. Touching the end of your spine and feeling the front of your pubis is also helpful to find these markers.

- As you inhale, image the breath moving down into your pelvic floor and expanding the distance between these boney points. The sitz bones and the tail and pubic bone will move apart from each other as the muscles of the pelvic floor open and expand outward. As you exhale, consciously bring the four points toward the center of the perineum so that they are closer together. You will feel a lifting and condensing of the pelvic floor muscles as they dome upward.

- Next, reverse this process by engaging and gently lifting the pelvic floor as you inhale (your thoracic diaphragm will still be widening downward on the inhalation) and releasing it on the exhalation. Your two diaphragms will be moving toward each other on the inhalation and away from each other on the exhalation.[87]

- After exploring these two ways of connecting your breathing to your pelvic floor, let go of actively engaging the diaphragm muscles with the breath and sit with a sense of aliveness, tone, and vitality that is at the base of your support.

- The pelvic floor can be imagined as a nicely stretched and toned drum skin that is not too tight and not too loose. Sometimes it is helpful to actively engage these muscles, condensing and expanding energetically to find the "not too tight, not too loose" sweet spot of relaxation and vitality.

Sensory Focus

- When you activate the pelvic floor, the support and tone you feel can express itself through your whole body. Notice whether, when you connect the pelvic floor to your breathing process, there is a natural deepening and aliveness that moves through your groin and down through your legs.

Contemplation

- The area of the pelvic floor can be a sensitive place to explore because of its association with sexuality and the bodily functions of elimination. Proceed gently and be mindful and respectful of feelings that arise as you bring your awareness to these tissues.

Two other areas of the body with fibers that run horizontally in the body are the *vocal* and *cranial* diaphragms. The vocal diaphragm modulates the pressure and tension in the vocal cords to produce sound, while the *dura mater* or outer covering of the brain is a kind of skullcap that both protects and responds to internal cranial pressure. By visualizing a widening happening horizontally at the throat behind the Adam's apple and a spreading in the cranial diaphragm, you can contribute to developing core support for the neck and head. Through the pelvic floor we connect to earth, our thoracic floor supports our torso, and our throat and skull allow us to reach toward the sky or heaven.

The quality of our breath is constantly changing, accurately reflecting our various activities and states of mind. As you go through your day, notice your breathing process and how it changes according to your emotional state, speediness, and physical activity. Tuning in to the breath can be a positive way to touch in with how you are feeling, emotionally and physically.

Part Three

Mindfulness of Body in
Everyday Life

12

Beyond the Physical Art of Sitting

"The process of embodiment entails initiating breath, movement, voice, awareness, and touch from any cell or collection of cells (as tissues and systems) and to witness what arises."

—Bonnie Bainbridge Cohen

At some point on our journey, we discover that we no longer need to continually monitor or reference our posture. When we sit down to meditate we feel fully embodied: our body and mind feel synchronized, our posture is aligned with gravity, and we feel basically grounded and supported. At this point in our development, we can relax and enjoy the posture as a natural expression of intelligence, spaciousness, and balance. This is the fruition of having deepened our relationship to the felt sense of the body and applied mindfulness to very specific aspects of our physical being.

It might seem counterintuitive, but by paying such close attention to our bodies, we actually end up with less fixation on all our physical aches, pains, stresses, strains, and postural imbalances. Our loving attention has succeeded in opening up the inner space of our bodies. Space is no longer only something outside of us and no longer do we exist purely as solid entities in that space. It is as if all the semipermeable membranes of the body allow life-force energy to blow right through us so that there is no longer such a sharp distinction between our inner and outer worlds.

At this point in our practice, spontaneous images and metaphors might arise that describe and enhance our experience. No longer dependent on using anatomical imagery of the body to change habitual patterns or to settle the mind, we can welcome images from our experience to further deepen our practice. A classic image in Tibetan Buddhist teachings describes the posture and practice of meditation as "sitting like a corpse, looking out, with eyes open." This describes a state of body-mind that emerged from the practice itself.

These are valuable self-instructions and they can be quite personal. I have imagined myself breathing into the middle space of my body, feeling into what I perceived as my "middle layers," when I immediately sensed a shift in perception. The inner space between my front and back opened up and with that opening, I felt expansive and accommodating. I was allowing myself the space I needed to just breathe and be.

Another time, when I noticed the natural warmth and energy spreading through my body, an image arose of a resting baby with a full belly, content and relaxed. When a student of mine meditates, she has an image of herself as a pine tree, with her roots spreading deep into the earth, a solid trunk, and full branches spreading and reaching toward the sky. You can celebrate the creativity of what arises out of your somatic explorations and the deepening connection to your body and your meditation practice.

13

The Four Postures of Meditation

"Within my body I have this incredible confidence—contentment, joy, equanimity, and wisdom."

—Sakyong Mipham

Bringing what you've been practicing on the cushion into your daily life will contribute presence and embodiment to everything you experience. As you listen to your body with greater sensitivity and awareness, the body begins to speak through powerful metaphors, stories, memories, or sudden insights. When we feel more with our physical bodies, invariably we experience the "emotional body" with all its richness, intelligence, and colorful expression. The information and insights we gain from fully feeling what we feel can open up new pathways to changing habits of body and mind. Many of the contemplations at the end of the guided practices encourage you to explore the psychological aspects of the somatic instructions in your daily life.

There are many ways to integrate your somatic meditation into your life activities. You might inquire into why an area of your body feels particularly stressed or unsupported. You might apply "mindfulness of body" to your daily movement activities.

While we have been primarily exploring the sitting posture of meditation, traditionally the Buddha recognized four ideal postures of meditation. Each of these postures provides a simple physical basis for the mind to settle into the practice of mindfulness and awareness. Each posture, from prone to sitting to standing to walking, elicits a different quality of being. The postures mirror a developmental process as we journey from a deeply internal state of yielding to gravity, to moving through space, to opening to our environment with our senses outwardly focused and engaged. These postures are the gestures or *mudras* of our daily lives and as such, they can act as a bridge from more formal meditation to post-meditation experience and meditation in action.

Lying Down

The chapter "Making Friends with Gravity" highlighted the importance of fully yielding to gravity to release excess tension in the body and cultivate the feeling of support that the earth provides for us. When we let down and lie down, we can fully surrender to this underlying, supporting surface. A bed, the floor, or even a grassy knoll all provide a supporting surface that holds us, grounds us, and nourishes us.

Sometimes we lie down while at the same time leaving our perception and awareness still sitting or standing. We might not be fully committed to letting go—perhaps we are still mentally finishing up at the office or constructing a to-do list. Synchronizing our mind with the posture of lying down is the first step in the meditative process.

A period of lying-down meditation can be particularly helpful when our bodies are in pain or we feel anxious and stressed. Follow the instructions in the guided exercise "Yielding." When your body feels like it has fully surrendered to gravity, bring your awareness to the sensations of your breathing or another object of meditation. When you lie down, it will be natural for the mind to begin to sink and for us to feel sleepy or start to daydream. If sleep is not your intention, pay special attention to your breathing process and keep your eyes open in order to remain present.

Lying on a relatively hard surface, like the floor or a yoga mat, will allow you to feel where your body meets the ground. This allows you to receive more feedback from your body as it begins to soften and relax. Here are recommended postures that support the ability to yield and release fully into gravity:

- Place a bolster or cushion underneath your knees so that your lower back is fully supported on the ground. If you tend to tip your chin toward the ceiling and shorten the back of your neck, adding a small pillow under your head or neck will be helpful.

- Constructive rest[88] is a posture designed to place your body in a position that takes the load off of habitually tight muscles. Lie on your back with your knees bent, feet turned slightly inward to allow your knees to touch. Your arms can lie by your sides or you can fold them across your chest, if that is comfortable.

- If your back is especially tight, lie on the floor with your feet and calves up on a chair. This is a wonderful way to let go of tension and deeply relax.

- If you are not used to lying directly on a hard surface such as the floor, it is fine to lie on your bed, just be mindful of the tendency to fall asleep. Simply follow the instructions in the "Yielding" exercise.

Integrating short periods of lying-down meditation into your daily life is easy. When you crawl into bed at night, a few minutes of meditation can act as a helpful sleep aid, offer a way to transition from daytime activity, and help you let go of the day's events. If you are about to begin a period of sitting meditation but feel especially anxious or your body is in distress, you can recuperate quite quickly with just a short, mindful rest on the ground.

Whether you choose to formally practice a period of meditation lying down, to bring awareness to the experience of lying down on your couch for a nap, or to relax in preparation for sleep, this is a posture you can continually return to for refreshment and renewal. At some point in our lives, due to injury, sickness, or the aging process, all of us will have the opportunity to practice meditation lying down.

Sitting

The most universal posture for meditation is the sitting posture. Sitting posture strikes a dynamic balance between the ability to focus inwardly and also maintain a connection to our environment. We are settled and grounded, yet focused and engaged.

We sit a lot. All of this sitting gives us many opportunities to utilize the principles and guided instructions in this book. We can notice how we sit at our computer, ride in our car, wait in a doctor's office, or sit down for dinner. Noticing the slump that happens in your office chair, you can reground yourself by locating a basis of support through the contact of your sitz bones and feet. You can realign your spinal curves and bring awareness to the very top of your spine where your skull sits. Feeling the opening or closing of your heart, or simply becoming aware of breathing in the lower lobes of your lungs, are all anatomical and physiological principles that can help you sit in any circumstance or condition, both on and off of the meditation cushion.

Standing

Standing meditation raises the energy level of your body-mind and can be done after walking meditation or between sessions of sitting meditation. Standing applies the same principles as sitting, except that the surface of support moves from your sitz bones to the soles of your feet. The supporting surface gets progressively smaller as you move from the ground, to sitting, to a standing posture, challenging you to balance the demand for increased muscular activity with ease and relaxation. The chapter "Making Friends with Gravity" describes the positive supporting reflexes that help inform your nervous system to actively recruit the muscles needed to resist gravity. When you engage the positive supporting reflexes of the feet,[89] there is a dynamic relationship with the earth. It counters the habit of locking your ankles, knees, and hip joints which—while temporarily making you feel stable and secure—sacrifices a flexible, awake, and relaxed connection with the earth.

Walking

The Shambhala Buddhist tradition offers four animal symbols that communicate the special qualities of skillful action.[90] Each animal expresses the quality that is manifested in both the body and mind of a master warrior meditator. Walking meditation is an opportunity for us to feel these qualities of movement and action in our bodies.

Guided Walking Meditation

Walk Like a Tiger—Mindfully place your soft tiger paws on the earth. Steady, gentle, and yielding. Release the weight of your body through your bones into the bones of your feet. Feel the subtle adjustments the bones of your feet need to make to accommodate your weight. Try walking without shoes, slowly enough that you can allow your feet to really feel the ground as they explore the terrain. You can engage the positive supporting reflexes as you walk, feeling the upward supporting surface of the earth meeting the bottoms of your feet as you tread softly but with strength.

Stride Like a Lion—Move your awareness to your belly and your pelvis. Feel the warmth and energy that is generated in this area through the processes of digestion and nutrition. Experience the natural joy that arises from feeling that you are a well-fed lion with lots of energy and a sense of buoyancy and lightness. With each step, move your pelvis fully over your supporting leg so that there is a sense of forward motion and a lack of hesitation in your step. You are not going anywhere in particular but each step moves you forward through space.

Glide Like a Garuda—Bring your awareness to your shoulders, arms, heart, and lungs. It can be helpful to fold one hand over the other and hold your hands near your navel. This hand mudra opens the shoulders and heart area while also connecting you to your center of gravity and support. Garudas are mythical creatures with wings: your garuda wings are folded but you can feel the openness across your chest. Feel the inspiration of your lungs and how your upper body just glides through space, riding on the movements of the lower body. Contact the openness and vulnerability of the heart moving forward in space. Feel the space around you that you are gliding in.

Gaze Like a Dragon—Feel your neck and beautifully balanced skull at the very top of your spine. Gaze out with soft eyes, receiving whatever you glide by without grasping. Extend your gaze in all directions so there is a sense of panoramic awareness and vision. Take it all in, but keep your mindful tiger paws moving steadily forward. Stay ordinary, walk without an agenda, and enjoy your connection with earth and sky.

By increasing your body awareness on and off the cushion, it is possible to gain a new confidence in which you trust the body's intelligence, experience the joy and pleasure that comes from bodily sensations, and feel the relaxation and contentment that comes with the body-mind connection.

14

Frequently Asked Questions

"Start where you are."
—Pema Chödrön

Q: I need to sit in a chair when I meditate, but I don't know what kind of chair is most supportive for practice. What do you recommend?

A: After decades of recliners, the furniture industry is beginning to design more supportive and orthopedically sound chairs. Depending on your physical limitations, you either want a chair that has a good lumbar support or, if you can sit upright without leaning back, you want a chair with a firm seat. You don't want to sink into the seat, as this will put pressure on your lower back and hips. Your feet should be flat on the floor, but if they don't reach you can put a firm cushion or other support under them. Unless you have the flexibility to maintain the curve in your lower back, your knees should always be either directly in line with your hips or slightly lower.

A meditation bench allows you to sit with your legs folded underneath you, making it somewhat easier to maintain the curve of your lower back. If you have knee problems, be sure you check that there is not undue stress on your knees, as the seat on a bench is tilted with more weight angled toward the knees.

Q: I almost always experience tension between my shoulder blades when I meditate. Why does this happen and what can I do?

A: First, explore the relationship of your head to your spine. If your head is not balanced properly on your first vertebra (the atlas), that imbalance can translate into shoulder and neck tension or pain. Second, notice if you have a proper lumbar curve. Is your lower back either too straight or overly curved? Third, make sure that the yoke of your shoulder girdle is properly aligned, with a special emphasis on releasing of the tips of your shoulder blades down your back. Fourth, tune into the organs and be curious about your heart and lungs. Can you feel and breathe into the back of your heart? Is your heart dropped forward or is it retreating against the back ribs? If so, visualize the vertical axis of the heart and feel the bottom resting on the horizontal platform of the diaphragm. Can you breathe into all the lobes of the lungs? Breathing into each lobe will support and massage different parts of your back.

Q: After just a short time sitting in the meditation posture, my feet and sometimes my legs fall asleep. Why does this happen and how can I prevent it?

A: This usually means that some of the nerves that enervate the lower body are becoming constricted, which cuts off some of the circulation to the legs and feet. Sometimes just changing your position by placing the other leg in front for a while can release the constriction, but if it continues to bother you, try placing a rolled-up towel or other form of soft support under your ankles or lower legs and knees. You will need to experiment with placing soft props under different areas to achieve the best undersurface support for your structure. Alleviate any acute angles, especially at the ankle joints.

Q: When I focus on the breath in meditation practice, my breathing often feels tight and sometimes I can't even feel my breath. Do you have any suggestions?

A: This is a common problem, especially when people first begin meditation practice. Although it can be very helpful to bring awareness to the breathing process by working directly with the diaphragm and the lungs, often in the beginning it is more effective to work with balancing your posture for optimal support. As your body begins to relax, the breath comes more naturally. I also suggest that you practice the exercise "Cellular Breathing" so that you begin to experience whole-body breathing. Because our normal breath patterns are usually unconscious, yet reveal our state of mind, when we are asked to place our awareness on the breath we can feel self-conscious or even resist the practice. By becoming familiar with the more subtle approach of the cellular breathing practice, we lessen the self-consciousness and eventually our normal breath pattern becomes more natural and effortless.

Q: Since I began sitting regularly I have become aware of all the imbalances in my body. I'm not sure how to deal with this newfound awareness. I feel uncomfortable.

A: When we slow down, we notice more. In the same way that we often feel that our mind is even more filled with discursive thought than before we began meditating, we also notice every ache, pain, and imbalance of the body as our body-awareness increases. You can celebrate your awareness and ability to feel more, even when it is uncomfortable, because this is the ground for change. If you get hooked into thinking about how everything is out of whack and what a mess you are, you will only remove yourself from the direct experience of body sensation. It is the willingness to be with the actual experience, and not what you think about it, that allows change to occur. If you can simply notice what you notice and stay with the feeling and not the commentary, you will begin to relax and soften. Then the imbalances and discomfort lessens. This doesn't mean that you can't apply the techniques in this book to work with the habitual body patterns you have noticed, but there is a delicate balance between obsessing over "problems" and yielding into what is. Often, it is the self-judgments and subtle resistance to what we feel that is blocking us from real change.

Q: When I sit down to meditate, I feel so antsy and uncomfortable in my body. It's really hard to sit still. Any suggestions?

A: Many people find it very helpful to do a few stretches or a bit of movement practice before sitting down to meditate. You could also begin a session with the "Yielding" exercise, which is done lying down. Although if you are tired, lying down might not be as helpful as stretching or a doing few minutes of aerobic exercise. By moving before sitting in meditation, you make a gentle transition into recontacting your body and releasing some of the holding and kinks that tend to build up during the day's activities. If you practice various visualizations and somatic exercises offered in this book and learn to resonate with the inner, subtler movement of your body, eventually it will be possible to make a seamless transition to the stillness of the meditation posture. You can learn to relax on the spot and at will.

Q: I seem to have a hard time figuring out where my center of balance is. Sometimes I notice that I am listing forward when I meditate, other times I feel that I'm pulling up and back. How can I go about finding the right spot?

A: First, establish your seat through the sitz bones and the pelvic floor. Remember that your central or vertical axis is an imaginary line that passes through the center of your body from the top of your head to the center of your pelvis—while it passes through the spine at different points, your axis is not your spine since the spine has four curves. Find the reference points for your alignment, so that your shoulders are directly over your hips and your head is in line with your shoulders. When you adjust your posture, or vertical axis, forward or backward only move from your hip sockets so that your central axis stays in line. If we are too forward or back, we tend to adjust our posture by either lifting or dropping the chest and rounding or arching our lower backs. Find the "plumb line" through your body and then practice bringing that plumb line forward a bit from the hips or back a bit until you feel that you are balanced right in the center of your pelvic floor and out the top of your head.

Q: I am an older meditator and when I get up from sitting I feel incredibly stiff. Is there anything I can do to relieve this feeling?

A: As we age, the fluid content of the body lessens. Most of our major joints contain *synovial fluid* for lubrication, but the aging process can thin the synovial membranes, making for stiffness and even pain in the major weight-bearing joints of the knees, hips, and ankles. Synovial fluid is stimulated at the joint capsule through movement of the joint. This is a major reason movement is so critical as we age. We literally need to oil our joints by moving them. So, after a prolonged meditation in relative stillness, we will feel stiff. One method is to move while meditating and adjust your posture, even minimally. Cross or uncross your legs and stretch a leg out for a moment. The more you move in small increments, the longer you will be able to meditate without "freezing over." When you finish practicing, you can stimulate the synovial fluid by shaking your joints out. Stretch your legs out in front of you and roll your legs in and out, stimulating the lubrication in the hip sockets before you even get up. When you come to standing, shake out your ankle joints, knees, hands, elbows, and shoulder joints. You can also wiggle up and down your spine. The shaking motion helps release the bones and joints and lubricate them.

15

Basic Meditation Instruction

"Body like a mountain
Breath like the wind
Mind like the sky"
—Tibetan wisdom conveyed by Ken McLeod

I offer these instructions as a guideline for those of you who have not been introduced to the formal practice of meditation. It is always best to seek out experienced instructors or teachers to support your practice but one can begin in a simple way. There are three basic components to meditation practice: posture, awareness of your breath, and noticing your thoughts.

- Decide on your sitting arrangement, either on a meditation cushion or chair, and settle into your posture, applying any somatic guidelines or contemplations that support you.

- Take a few moments to settle into your body and shift your awareness and sensation to your breathing process. The feeling of your breath is a tangible, bodily sensation as well as an intangible experience of spaciousness as your breath fills your body and then dissolves into your environment.

- Without manipulating your breath, simply notice your breath as it is in this very moment.

- Notice what you notice and feel what you feel. This is an opportunity to experience the movement, creativity, energy, and power of your thought process—while at the same time continually returning to the feeling of breathing.

- Awareness of your breath is an anchor to the present moment, allowing you to continually let go of elaborate storylines and distractions of all kinds. When you notice you have forgotten the breath, you can simply return to breath-awareness without comment or judgment.

- The meditation practice is a practice of noticing your thoughts, as they are, recognizing them as thinking, and then gently bringing your attention back to the sensation and feeling of the process of breathing.

Parting Thoughts

"When you sit erect, you are proclaiming to yourself and to the rest of the world that you are going to be a warrior, a fully human being."

—Chögyam Trungpa

It seems so simple: sit down, sit up straight, cross your legs, and practice being mindful of something. And yet, as Sakyong Mipham is fond of saying, simple is complicated. Our relationship with our body and mind can be deep and fathomless or relatively superficial. The depth does not depend on learning all there is to know about anatomy and structure or studying all there is to know about how our brain and mind work. Rather, it is the willingness to be totally present with our body-mind.

The practice of meditation and body awareness is a deep and profound practice of cultivating presence. All of the somatic practices and guided instructions in this book are for the sole purpose of cultivating this relaxed, awake presence. If our physical alignment is compromised or we have not yet found the right balance of effort and release in our posture, then it is more difficult to let go of our fixation on ego's desires, biases, judgments, and everything that makes up the "me plan." If our body feels constricted, it is constantly reminding us that we are bounded, material creatures that need constant coddling and attention. Like a needy child, our bodies distract us rather than liberate us.

By attending to the very basic needs of the body—to align our structure with gravity, to release what needs to be released, and to support what needs to be supported—we can turn our attention to the development of compassionate hearts and insightful minds. This is not to forget or ignore the body; it is to bring the body and mind into a state of harmony and union that no longer fights and struggles with the body-mind split. This is one of the purposes for doing basic meditation practice altogether.

In this book, I hope you have discovered some techniques, images, and suggestions that appeal to your individual learning style. If your body-awareness has grown, if you feel more confident and settled in your body, if you have learned new ways to alleviate unnecessary tension, and if you feel more relaxed in the posture of meditation, then you have successfully embarked on a lifetime journey of discovery. May your curiosity be unbounded and your meditation practice strengthened for many years to come.

Acknowledgments

I never set out to write a book but, somehow, it happened. It happened because of the encouragement and support of so many amazing and generous people. I first want to thank my husband, the wonderful Wendell Beavers, whose love and insight continue to sustain me; our son, Kai Beavers, who encouraged me throughout the process, offering support and early editorial assistance; and my sisters, brothers-in-law, and dear friends, who never seemed to have a doubt that I could do it. I also want to thank my early readers for their kind and thoughtful feedback: Cynthia Kneen, Chris Stockinger, Lucrezia Funghini, David Rome, Gary Allen, and Jules Levinson. Other contributors and supporters who I wish to thank with much gratitude are: Kathrin Scheel-Ungerleider, Agness Au, Clio Pavlantis, the Schwartz family, my amazing editor Jennifer Holder; designers Claire Crevey and Gail Nelson; and the talented artist Lydia Kegler, whose illustrations add so much beauty and clarity to the text. Finally, this book would never have been possible without the many students of meditation and all their feedback throughout the years I've been teaching. I am especially grateful for all the Shambhala Centers and Naropa University where I was given opportunities to freely explore the connections between somatics and meditation practice. May their generosity bring much benefit!

Notes

1. See Sakyong Mipham, *Turning the Mind Into an Ally*.

2. This movement is sometimes referred to as the "Human Potential Movement" and its creative center was the Esalen Institute in Big Sur, CA.

3. See Thomas Hanna, *What is Somatics?*, 1

4. Body-Mind Centering® is a registered service mark of Bonnie Bainbridge Cohen. See http://www.bodymindcentering.com.

5. Don Hanlon Johnson. *Body, Spirit, and Democracy*, 213.

6. Linda Hartley, *Wisdom of the Body Moving*, xxvii.

7. Tenzin Wangyal Rinpoche: "It is important to emphasize the distinction between the conceptual mind and the nature of mind, which I refer to as open awareness. We do not need to think in order to be aware. And awareness is not thinking." *Awakening the Sacred Body*, xvii.

8. Bonnie Bainbridge Cohen, *Sensing, Feeling, and Action*, vii.

9. Cyndi Dale, *The Subtle Body*, 3, 235, xxii.

10. See Lulu E. Sweigard, *Human Movement Potential*, 7

11. Sensory nerves bring information to the central nervous system (brain and spinal cord) and motor nerves that exit the central nervous system, allowing us to respond to that information.

12. See T.H. Mulder, "Motor Imagery and Action Observation: Cognitive Tools for Rehabilitation," *Journal of Neural Transmission*, 114, no. 10 (October 2007): 1265-1278.

13. Sports psychology research has shown that visualizing an action pathway and the subsequent desired goal of that action readily coordinates the neuromuscular details of the movement (the muscular recruitment, sequencing, timing, and force requirements). See Tony Morris, Michael Spittle, and Anthony P. Watt, *Imagery in Sport*.

14. Although the neuromuscular system has been the prime focus in idiokinetic practices in Body-Mind Centering, visualization is applied to all the tissues and systems of the body.

15. Cohen, *Sensing, Feeling, and Action*, 1.

16. The cerebral cortex is the primary intellectual processing area of the brain.

17. Cohen, *Sensing, Feeling, and Action*, 157.

18. Chögyam Trungpa, *The Path of Individual Liberation*, 276-278.

19. Chögyam Trungpa, *Shambhala: The Sacred Path of the Warrior*, 40.

20. For further instruction on contemplative practice, see Sakyong Mipham, *Turning the Mind into an Ally*, 227.

21. Will Johnson, *The Posture of Meditation*, 52.

22. Chögyam, Trungpa. *The Heart of the Buddha*, 31.

23. A reflex is a quick, involuntary response to a stimulus. Our basic movement patterns are made up of reflexes and nervous system responses that become integrated in the first few years of life.

24. This is the *tonic labrynthine reflex*, so named because it is within the labyrinths of the inner ear that forces of gravity are first registered by the low brain. Jean Ayres, *Sensory Integration and the Child*, 35.

25. Ibid., 62

26. You can also try laying on your belly with a pillow under your pelvis to support your lower back.

27. Cohen, *Sensing, Feeling, and Action,* 127.

28. Ibid., 132.

29. If you are used to holding your hands in a different position when you meditate, take note that wherever your hands make contact with your thighs becomes the underlying surface of support. You can still yield and gently push into that supporting surface.

30. This is an exercise once popular in etiquette training for "proper posture," yet it is still quite effective in waking up the positive supporting reflexes of the head.

31. Mabel Todd, *The Thinking Body*, 54.

32. Deane Juhan, *Job's Body,* 94.

33. Because the breathing diaphragm is connected through fascia and ligament to the front of the spine, our breathing moves the

spine as the diaphragm widens and lowers and then releases in the breathing process.

34. The *plumb line* or *vertical axis* is an imaginary line that passes through the center of the body from head to feet, determining an even distribution of weight or gravity around this vertical axis.

35. A pattern that emerges after birth, when the infant primarily moves in a worm-like motion from its tail to its head. See Cohen, *Sensing, Feeling, and Action,* 5

36. Todd, *The Thinking Body,* 157.

37. Chögyam Trungpa was fond of telling his students to "find your head and shoulders" as a way to uplift both their posture and their state of mind.

38. If you do this standing, take note if the palms of your hands are facing the sides of your body. When shoulders habitually roll forward, the palms tend to face backward.

39. In the sixteenth century, Vesalius named this vertebra that supports the head the "atlas" after the Greek god who supported the heavens on his shoulders.

40. Cohen, *Sensing, Feeling, and Action,* 3.

41. The *enteric nervous system* or "gut brain" is now considered part of the autonomic nervous system. We've all felt this connection when we feel "butterflies" in our gut with feelings of anxiety or insecurity. See Cohen, *Sensing, Feeling and Action,* 180.

42. See chapter 11, "The Life Force: Our Breath."

43. See chapter 8, "Exquisite Sensitivity: Our Nervous System," and

chapter 9, "Energetic Essence: Our Glands."

44. John Sarno was one of the first physicians to recognize the relationship between stress and lower back pain. See John Sarno, *Healing Back Pain: The Body-mind Connection.*

45. See Mimi Guarneri, *The Heart Speaks,* xi

46. This is the "positive supporting reflex" referred to on page 43.

47. Cohen, *Sensing, Feeling, and Action,* 3.

48. Hartley, *Wisdom of the Body Moving,* 256.

49. Ibid., 249.

50. Although we are primarily using the terminology of Western anatomy to cultivate body-mind balance in the sitting posture, I want to mention sacred or subtle anatomy in reference to the nervous system. Asian systems of medicine and yoga refer to a system of invisible channels that run through the body, called *nadis.* According to this system, our awareness and thought patterns ride on *prana,* "wind" or "breath," through these channels. The network of nerves and spinal-cord nerve tracts is not unlike this system, although the subtle-body anatomy is considered immaterial and invisible to the naked eye. Chögyam Trungpa described the tantric system in this way: "The nadi principle is connected with the channels in the body ... which provide communication from the top of our head to the soles of our feet. Nadis refer to the systems that relate and transmit messages constantly. If you put your finger on a hot plate, your brain picks that up. This kind of message and telecommunication system that goes through the body is called nadis" (Trungpa,

The Tantric Path of Indestructible Wakefulness). Exciting new research is investigating the relationship of nerves to the invisible meridians that are the basis of acupuncture and Traditional Chinese Medicine. The initial findings point to energy related to the different organs and parts of the body flowing along the same pathways as many of the major nerves.

51. The sensory nerves enter the back of the spinal cord, while the motor nerves exit out the front of the cord.

52. Bonnie Bainbridge Cohen refers to this as allowing the information "to find the easy path." In other words, you don't necessarily need to be responsible for how sensory information is perceived; the sound of a bell can be just that, a sound.

53. Shambhala Buddhism uses the traditional analogy of a tiger or a lion walking mindfully through the jungle or resting quietly— yet completely focused and alert.

54. The retina is not a peripheral sensory organ like the skin's touch receptors or the tongue's taste buds. Rather, it is an outgrowth of central nervous tissue. Because of this origin, the retina has layers of neurons, internal circuits, and transmitters that are characteristic of the brain. It is a bit of the brain that has journeyed out, literally, to have a look at the environment.

55. Barbara Dilley, a longtime Naropa University faculty member, refers to this eye practice as the discovery of your "infant eyes." See Barbara Dilley, *This Very Moment*, 122-124.

56. Bainbridge Cohen and others have suggested that the hypothalamus and the limbic area deep within the center of the

brain are the keystones of this endocrine and nervous system connection. See Cohen, *Sensing, Feeling, and Action*, 57, and Hartley, *Wisdom of the Body Moving*, 221.

57. New research is proposing that females in particular, can react to stress through a "tend and befriend" response—perhaps based in part on the oxytocin hormone. See http://www.ncbi.nlm.nih.gov/pubmed/10941275 and Cohen, *Sensing, Feeling and Action*, 183.

58. Candace Pert and other neuroscientists have been researching how these substances (along with a wider category of molecules called *peptides*) carry "information" throughout the body. They could provide a possible scientific explanation for how the mind is expressed throughout the body and ultimately, not "located" solely within the brain itself. Pert and other neuroscientists call these molecules "informational substances," since they are messenger molecules that distribute information throughout the organism. According to Pert, the information they are carrying is primarily emotional—hence her reference to these as "molecules of emotion." See Candace Pert, *Molecules of Emotion*.

59. Hartley, *Wisdom of the Body Moving*, 207.

60. For further information on the gland and chakra connection, read Linda Hartley's *Wisdom of the Body Moving* and Bonnie Bainbridge Cohen's *Sensing, Feeling, and Action*.

61. Hartley, *Wisdom of the Body Moving*, 211.

62. Bonnie Bainbridge Cohen refers to tissues that appear to secrete chemicals that have not been identified as *bodies*. The definitions

of what is or is not a gland are changing rapidly. For instance, the heart and gut were recently found to have glandular tissue.

63. In a discussion on the first chakra (located variably at either the center of the perineum or at the end of the spine) and the importance of understanding form and physical manifestation, Chögyam Trungpa said, "The earth-bounding quality, the quality which is connected with the earth and solidity—that is the basic essence of spirituality." *Secret Beyond Thought*, 2.

64. The perineal body is also referred to as the *central tendon of the perineum*.

65. Bonnie Bainbridge Cohen, "The Neuroendocrine System" (unpublished paper, The School for Body-Mind Centering, Amherst, Massachusetts).

66. Contemporary yogis sometimes refer to this gland as the *kundalini* gland, a reference to the "coiled serpent" of spiritual energy that yogis believe rests at the base of the spine, waiting to be activated by the yoga of tantric practitioners. See Janna Dixon, *The Biology of Kundalini.*

67. The image of Leonardo Da Vinci's "Vitruvian Man" expresses the centrality of the solar plexus and its relationship to the end points of the body in space.

68. The heart was designated as an endocrine gland in 1983. See Guarneri, *The Heart Speaks,* 156.

69. Ibid.,155.

70. Bonnie Bainbridge Cohen, *Embodied Anatomy: The Endocrine System* (CA: Burchfield Rose, 2016), DVD.

71. In embryological development, all of the head glands grow out of the hypothalamus.

72. Glandular excretions affect our body-mind function in a feedback loop via the nervous system. The stimulation or inhibition of any one gland affects all the others. This is why in major glandular shifts, like puberty or menopause, every system in the body and mind is affected.

73. Hartley, *Wisdom of the Body Moving*, 268

74. Cohen, *Sensing, Feeling, and Action*, 67.

75. See Chögyam Trungpa, *The Path of Individual Liberation,* 323

76. Cohen, *Sensing, Feeling, and Action*, 70.

77. There is also growing evidence that some of the CSF leaves the spinal canal via the spinal nerves or within the connective tissue and travels throughout the body, some of it eventually being absorbed into the interstitial fluid. See: Juhan's *Job's Body,* 73; Harley's *Wisdom of the Body Moving,* 281.

78. Cohen, *Sensing, Feeling, and Action*, 79.

79. "Meditation is the natural process of becoming familiar with an object by repeatedly placing our minds on it." Sakyong Mipham, *Turning the Mind Into an Ally*, 24.

80. Particular yogic exercises might emphasize deep breathing and manipulation of the diaphragm.

81. "Cellular presence" refers to the experience of simply resting your mind within the fluid of the cell. This is in contrast to "cellular breathing," which is the experience of the subtle movement or pulsing of the cellular membranes as the fluid carrying oxygen

and carbon dioxide enters and leaves the cells.

82. In Body-Mind Centering, the vocal folds and the fibrous outer "skin" that covers the top and bottom of the brain—called the *dura*—are also explored as diaphragms.

83. See *Divry's Modern English-Greek and Greek-English Dictionary*, s.v. "diaphragm."

84. The horizontal plane is sometimes referred to as the "table plane" in somatic movement. It refers to movement happening in relationship to gravity that is horizontal, like a table.

85. Bainbridge Cohen has suggested that some of the diaphragms' fibers also run upward along the front of the spine, lending support to the whole length of the spine.

86. Bonnie Bainbridge Cohen refers to these two diaphragms as functionally *one* diaphragm, citing the relationship between the rectus abdominus in front, from pubis to sternum, the central crura of the thoracic diaphragm running along the front of the spine to the tailbone and then blending into the pelvic floor, and the external and internal oblique muscles that wrap around the sides of the body and knit into the rectus. See Bonnie Bainbridge Cohen, *Embodied Anatomy: The Axial Skeleton*, Disc 3, Chapter 1 (CA: Burchfield Rose, 2016), DVD.

87. The practice of bringing the two diaphragms toward each other on the inhalation and away from each other on the exhalation is common to many yogic and Taoist practices. My purpose is to simply offer ways to bring tone to the pelvic floor along with the

invitation to explore the physical and emotional qualities of these different ways of breathing.

88. "Constructive rest" is a position codified by somatic educators Mabel Todd and Lulu Sweigard. See Sweigard, *Human Movement Potential,* chapter on "Constructive Rest," 215-221.

89. See page 43 for instructions on engaging the positive supporting reflexes of the feet.

90. For an in-depth contemplation on the Four Dignities, see chapter 21 in Sakyong Mipham's *Ruling Your World.*

Bibliography

Ayres, Jean. *Sensory Integration and the Child*. Torrance, CA: Western Psychological Services, 1979.

Cohen, Bonnie Bainbridge. *Embodied Anatomy,* DVD sets. CA: Burchfield Rose, 2016.

Cohen, Bonnie Bainbridge. *Sensing, Feeling, and Action: The Experiential Anatomy of Body-Mind Centering*. Northampton, MA: Contact Editions, 2008.

Conrad, Emilie. *Life on Land: The Story of Continuum, the World-Renowned Self-Discovery and Movement Method*. Berkeley, CA: North Atlantic Books, 2007.

Dale, Cyndi. *The Subtle Body: An Encyclopedia of Your Energetic Anatomy*. Boulder, CO: Sounds True, 2009.

Dilley, Barbara. *This Very Moment: Teaching Thinking Dancing*. Boulder: Naropa University Press, 2015.

Dixon, Janna. *The Biology of Kundalini*. Website version, 2006. http://biologyofkundalini.com.

Frankl, Viktor E. *Man's Search for Meaning*. 4th ed. Boston: Beacon Press, 2000.

Franklin, Eric. *Dynamic Alignment Through Imagery*. Champagne, IL: Human Kinetics, 1996.

Guarneri, Mimi. *The Heart Speaks: A Cardiologist Reveals the Secret Language of Healing*. New York: Touchstone, 2006.

Hartley, Linda. *Wisdom of the Body Moving*. Berkeley: North Atlantic, 1989.

Hanna, Thomas. "What is Somatics?" *Somatics: Magazine-Journal of the Bodily Arts and Sciences* 5, no. 4 (Spring-Summer 1986): 4–8.

Johnson, Don Hanlon. *Body, Spirit, and Democracy*. Berkeley: North Atlantic, 1994.

Johnson, Will. *The Posture of Meditation: A Practical Manual for Meditators of All Traditions*. Boston & London: Shambhala, 1996.

Juhan, Deane. *Job's Body: A Handbook for Bodywork*. Barrytown, NY: Station Hill, 2003.

Kapit, Wynn, and Lawrence M. Elson. *The Anatomy Coloring Book*. San Francisco: Benjamin Cummings, 2002.

McLeod, Ken. *Wake Up to Your Life*. San Francisco: HarperOne, 2002.

Mipham, Sakyong. *Turning the Mind Into an Ally*. New York: Riverhead, 2003.

Mipham, Sakyong. *Ruling Your World: Ancient Strategies for Modern Life*. New York: Morgan Road, 2005.

Morris, Tony, Michael Spittle, and Anthony P. Watt. *Imagery in Sport*. Champagne, IL: Human Kinetics, 2005.

Pert, Candace B. *Molecules of Emotion: The Science Behind Body-mind Medicine*. New York: Scribner, 1997.

Sarno, John. *Healing Back Pain: The Body-mind Connection*. New York: Warner Books, 1991.

Suzuki, Shunryu. *Zen Mind, Beginner's Mind*. New York & Tokyo: Weatherhill Books, 1970.

Sweigard, Lulu E. *Human Movement Potential: Its Ideokinetic Facilitation*. New York: Harper & Row, 1974.

Todd, Mabel E. *The Thinking Body*. New York: Dance Horizons, 1937.

Trungpa, Chögyam. *The Heart of the Buddha*. Boston & London: Shambhala, 1991.

Trungpa, Chögyam. *The Path of Individual Liberation*. Vol. 1, *The Profound Treasury of the Ocean of Dharma*. Boulder, CO: Shambhala, 2013.

Trungpa, Chögyam. *Secret Beyond Thought.* Halifax, NS: Vajradhatu, 1991.

Trungpa, Chögyam. *Shambhala: The Sacred Path of the Warrior.* Boulder, CO: Shambhala, 1984.

Trungpa, Chögyam. *The Tantric Path of Indestructible Wakefulness.* Vol. 3, The Profound Treasury of the Ocean of Dharma. Boulder, CO: Shambhala, 2013.

Wangyal, Tenzin. *Awakening the Sacred Body: Tibetan Yogas of Breath and Movement.* Carlsbad, CA: Hay House, 2011.

Further Reading

Aposhyan, Susan. *Natural Intelligence.* Boulder: NOW Press, 2007.

Calais-Germain, Blandine. *Anatomy of Movement.* Seattle: Eastland Press, 1993.

Clemente, Carmine D. *Anatomy: A Regional Atlas of the Human Body.* Philadelphia: Lea & Febiger, 1975.

Olsen, Andrea. *Body and Earth: An Experiential Guide.* Hanover: UPNE, 2002.

Olsen, Andrea. *Body Stories: A Guide to Experiential Anatomy.* Barrytown NY: Station Hill, 1991.

About the Author

Erika Berland is a member of a pioneering generation of somatic movement educators. As a certified practitioner of Body-Mind Centering, a licensed massage therapist, and registered movement therapist, she has a long and distinguished career in the fields of the performing arts, movement, and massage therapy. She has made significant contributions to the integration of dance, physical theater, and contemplative practice within somatic education and continues to teach and present at conferences nationally and internationally. She is a founding faculty member and co-creator of the unique movement curriculum of the MFA Theater: Contemporary Performance Program at Naropa University, where she has been at the forefront of creating new techniques and applications of Bonnie Bainbridge Cohen's groundbreaking work in Body-Mind Centering. She was instrumental in the development of the first application of movement analysis to fitness, and enhancing performance, at the Sports Training Institute and Plus One Fitness Center in New York City. Erika was an early student of the meditation master and founder of Naropa University, Chögyam Trungpa, and is a senior teacher of meditation in the Shambhala Buddhist tradition. Additional publications include a chapter in *Movement for Actors*

(Allworth Press 2017) titled "Somatic Training for Actors with the Principles of Body-Mind Centering" and a chapter in *Physical Dramaturgy* (Routledge Press 2017), titled "A Dramaturgy of Embodiment; Accessing the Expressivity of the Body Through the Study and Practice of Experiential Anatomy."

Made in the USA
San Bernardino, CA
19 March 2017